What people have said

HR Professionals

"*Peace at Work* is a must-read for all HR professionals who aspire to a better solution to workplace conflict and who want to add the skill of mediation to their toolbox. John Ford takes a lifetime of mediation knowledge and presents it in an easy-to-understand, step-by-step process, from opening statements to closing agreements and every step in between."

Todd Clawson, MS
Director of Human Resources, Parker County Hospital District

"In *Peace at Work*, John clearly lays out an effective path to resolving conflict in the workplace. I especially appreciate the emphasis on how mediators should prepare themselves to impart peace by maintaining a stance that is open and present in the moment. John explains that 'we are honored guests in the intimate lives of the participants with whom we work'. The book is infused with reverence for all aspects of workplace mediation and is a wonderful guide to the process as a whole."

Wayne Seeley
Human Resources Professional

"Practical, visionary and strategic. John's book should be a resource on the desk of every HR professional and of anyone who manages people. He leads you through the why, how, when and what to do to help people get through conflicts so they can get back to work, and you can too! *Peace at Work*, accessible and inspiring, can help you not only to help others resolve their conflicts, but to build a stronger and more trusting work environment in the process."

Rita Sever
Supervision Matters

HR Managers (who have trained and worked with the author)

"I have worked with John on various mediations over the years. He cares deeply about the people involved in his mediations and this is reflected in his consummate application of the skills and strategies in *Peace at Work*. This book is a natural complement to, and an excellent compilation of, John's considerable store of knowledge about mediation in the workplace."

Beth Delaney
Human Resource Business Partner, Kaiser Permanente

"*Peace at Work* is a true guide for HR professionals. I had the pleasure of attending one of John Ford's seminars and was amazed by his insights regarding how early recognition of workplace conflict can lead to resolution. John is a natural trainer with a sense of humor, and his book is a true testament to his gifted mediation skills. I recommend this book to anyone looking to master the skills of internal workplace mediation."

Shelly Singh
Human Resource Professional

"I had the pleasure of taking a mediation course led by John Ford. He was a truly inspiring teacher and his course proved immediately useful in my work in labor and employee relations. Many of the wise insights John shared with us in class are included in *Peace at Work*. HR and other managers looking for clear and practical advice about how to conduct a mediation will find it here, and will be better able to see why mediation is potentially so effective in resolving conflict."

Maryl Olivera,
Labor and Employee Relations (retired), Administrative Office of the Courts

"John Ford's book, *Peace at Work*, will help any manager or HR professional to successfully mediate conflict. Mr Ford draws from his vast personal experience and insight, as well as that of many experts in the field, in this well-written and well-organized book. He covers foundational concepts and provides a structured approach to what is an easy-to-use, step-by-step model for mediation. Complete with case-study role-plays and a rich appendix of supporting materials and reference listings, the book is a must for anyone who leads people."

Peter Haralabopoulos
Flight Attendant Base Director, San Francisco International Airport

Other Authors

"John Ford offers a lucid and highly practical introduction to workplace mediation which incorporates key insights regarding managing conflict communications and emotions. *Peace at Work* is a 'go to' reference for HR managers who want to improve their organization's ability to manage conflicts and disputes."

Craig E. Runde
Director, Center for Conflict Dynamics and Mediation Training Institute
Co-author (with T.A. Flanagan) of *Becoming a Conflict Competent Leader: How You and Your Organization can Manage Conflict Effectively*

"John Ford has written a useful and important book on workplace conflict, designed specifically for HR professionals. It offers sound practical advice, important insights into workplace conflict and the mediation process, and a unique perspective on conflict communication and the quality of 'presence' which we ought to bring to our work. I recommend it highly, not only for HR managers, but also for workplace mediators and anyone who would like to know how the process works."

Kenneth Cloke
Author of *Resolving Conflicts at Work: Ten Strategies for Everyone on the Job*

"John Ford's conception of the mediator's stance is pure genius, and an important contribution to the field. He approaches mediation from the inside out, which is exactly right. If there were ever a shortcut to mediation mastery – in the workplace or anywhere else – this is it."

Eileen Barker
Author of *Forgiveness Workbook: A Step by Step Guide*

"John Ford embodies many of the values the conflict-resolution field holds dear: active listening, emotional intelligence and open-heartedness. Those traits are why he is such an effective mediator, and why he has such insight into workplace dynamics. This book, growing out of John's wisdom, will be an essential resource for all HR managers looking to build peace within their organizations."

Colin Rule
Author of *Online Dispute Resolution for Business: E-commerce, B2B, Consumer, Employment, Insurance, and other Commercial Conflicts*

Other Mediators

"The growing field of workplace mediation has lacked a comprehensive best practices guide. In *Peace at Work*, John Ford – long-time mediator and former managing editor at Mediate.com – offers HR professionals an indispensable guide for workplace mediation. My prediction is that this book will rapidly become required reading for both workplace mediators and HR professionals."

Jim Melamed
CEO, Mediate.com

"This book is a simple yet elegant guide for the HR manager to enter the workplace mediation experience. Its arrival could not have come at a better time for organizations that have a desire to build their internal capacity to be conflict competent. John writes with clarity and passion. His writing is based on his extensive experience in the field and his desire to demystify a skill that every HR manager needs."

Carole Houk
Carole Houk International, LLC

"John Ford has followed his search for peace through the legal system and across the globe. He has seen the full spectrum of conflict: international human rights grievances, corporate system design, high-conflict divorce, and community justice disputes. He has combined this experience into one book with one goal: improving the workplace. John has a highly tuned intuition for bringing volatile, seemingly disparate people into a productive relationship. His book shows the clear process for addressing workplace conflict and gives advice on handling different types of conflict. It is a gift to HR managers."

Dr Clare Fowler
Managing Editor, Mediate.com

"Bravo, John Ford! *Peace at Work* is a masterful library-must-have for HR managers who want finger-on-the-pulse guidance to transcend and shift conflict in the workplace. The book humanizes best practices for authentic, restorative dialogue and promotes a safer, more civil environment in which HR managers can mediate with clarity in the understanding that they are where peace begins."

Steffi Berkowitz
CEO, Berkowitz Civility Group

"John Ford has captured the essence of workplace mediation. HR Managers will benefit from the sensible mediation knowledge which he shares. This book fills the gaps for HR managers by providing rational and unique ways of looking at conflict in the workplace, and by providing clear and wise options towards conflict resolution."

Ayan Ahmed
Freelance Journalist and Conflict Resolution Specialist

"John Ford's grasp of the dynamics of conflict and creative paths to resolution is second to none."

David D Stein, Esq.
Founder, Liaise Mediated Solutions LLC

Comments from Southern Africa

"In a workplace thwart with increasing conflict, more HR Managers are required to become peacemakers. John Ford's practical guide provides a systematic approach for achieving this outcome."

Kavena Hambira, MS HRM
Namibian Fullbright Scholar

"In *Peace at Work*, John achieves what many people with great minds struggle to do – share their knowledge and expertise simply yet profoundly. Using language that is easily understood and concepts that can be quickly grasped and replicated in practice, his book speaks universally to you and I as HR practitioners. Thanks, John, for taking the time to write it."

Gwynn Prickett
People Development Consultant and former HR Director, South Africa

"I have had the privilege of previewing *Peace at Work*. Having interacted with John over the years, I know enough to know that peacemaking is innate to him, and so it comes as no surprise that this is not your average dispute-resolution 'how to' manual. John has produced a brilliant work which pulls together solid mediation and peacemaking theory, drawing inspiration from his knowledge, experience, qualifications and mentors. But the work stands out in its ability to convey brilliantly the intuitive side of peacemaking practice. Many could distinguish themselves in practice simply by understanding the majestic revelation intrinsic to the chapter 'The Mediator's Stance'. I think this work achieves excellence and I will certainly be recommending it as a resource to our students."

Sheena Jonker
Alternative Dispute Resolution Practitioner, Academic Lawyer and Human Rights Activist, ADR network South Africa and the Access to Justice Association of Southern Africa

Peace at Work

The HR Manager's Guide to Workplace Mediation

John Ford

John Ford
John Ford and Associates
(+1) 510 632 6192 (office)
(+1) 510 301 9095 (cell)
john@johnford.com
www.johnford.com
@TheHRmediator

Editor: Avrille du Plessis
Layout: Perri Caplan
Cover: Jane Sheppard

ISBN: 978-1500331351
ISBN-10: 150033135X

This book is dedicated to my parents.

Peace

*It does not mean to be in a place
where there is no noise, trouble
or hard work, it means to be in
the midst of those things and
still be calm in your heart.*

Unknown

Contents

Preface

"Imagine all the people, living life in peace..."
John Lennon

I was born in South Africa in 1962 during the infamous apartheid era. By the time I was at university studying law, I knew I wanted to be part of a new South Africa, although in truth I was not very hopeful.

After matriculating from school, I was drafted into the South African Air Force and spent six months on the 'border' in Namibia (or South West Africa, as it was then called). South Africa was illegally occupying Namibia in breach of an International Court of Justice (ICJ) ruling and was fighting a low-intensity war with the People's Liberation Army of Namibia (PLAN), who were based in Angola and supported militarily by Cuba. The situation seemed hopeless and it was hard to imagine how the regional and civil conflict would ever end.

At university, I involved myself in student politics. I was a member of the End Conscription Campaign and joined my fellow students in demanding the end to apartheid, and specifically the drafting into the armed forces of all white males. I hoped to use my law degree to be an advocate for justice, especially in the workplace, where labor and employment laws provided some opportunities to address a patently unfair system.

After graduating, I moved to Windhoek, Namibia, in 1988, to practice law with Lorentz & Bone. Founded in 1920, it was the largest and oldest law firm in Namibia. When I left, I was one of seven partners. I specifically wanted to work there as I knew they were doing most of the political human rights work in the country. I represented numerous victims of human rights abuses, including the San (Bushmen) of the Kalahari, and maintained a general practice that addressed divorce and labor law. Both of these areas of practice would, unbeknownst to me at the time, provide my first opportunities to mediate.

As a divorce attorney, I started inviting both spouses involved in the divorce to my office so we could focus on a reasonable settlement rather than fuel the fires of escalation. Together, we would work things out and allow the court to 'rubber stamp' the marital settlement agreement. As a labor attorney, I sat as chairperson on a number of conciliation boards appointed to resolve disputes between companies and their recognized unions.

At that time, I had received no formal mediation training. I remember meeting Johann van Rooyen, Director of Manpower in the then Department of Civic Affairs and Manpower (subsequently Namibia's Ministry of Labor), before the start of my first conciliation board. He took me aside and said that it sometimes helped to meet privately with the company in the morning and then with the union in the afternoon. I did that, and it helped. I know now that he was encouraging me to caucus, a topic I cover extensively in this book.

Then, in 1990, Nelson Mandela was released from prison, and Namibia obtained independence through the United Nations (UN) peace plan known as Resolution 435. The focus of my practice shifted from human rights work to labor and employment law. I became the 'go to' partner in our firm, and was eventually appointed the Law Society's member of the first Namibia Labor Courts' Rules Board. I still maintained a small divorce practice on the side.

At this time, I hosted a seminar for HR managers on the new labor laws that did away with the 'at will' employment doctrine in place in Namibia at the time. In essence, this doctrine had allowed termination on notice, without substantive reasons. It was replaced with a provision that was compliant with the International Labor Organization: all employment decisions had to follow a fair procedure and be substantively fair.

I litigated many unfair discipline and termination cases in the context of these procedural and substantive rights. Some settled in a mediation-like forum with a labor inspector, really a settlement conference that our then new labor court rules mandated before trial. Others went the costly way of trial.

Some of the more interesting work I did was in the fishing industry. After Namibian independence, Pescanova was the biggest investor in the fishing industry and built a large factory at the coastal town of

Lüderitz. I helped them to negotiate their first collective bargaining agreement with the Namibia Food and Allied Workers Union (Nafau), and set the standard for how exemptions to the Labor Act were negotiated to address employment conditions while fishing at sea.

I was also involved in a crisis with another fishing company when the contract negotiator was held hostage by angry workers who threatened his life if their terms were not accepted. Police intervention saved the day, but the question of the derailed negotiations remained. Here is how Sigurdur Bogason, the then CEO of the National Fishing Corporation of Namibia Limited, and an Iceland expatriate, described my role:

Sitting under a siege situation a whole day with my labor negotiator taken hostage by between one to two hundred disgruntled employees (mainly lobster fishermen), facing threats of guns and rampant violence, it was a relief to learn that a labor dispute expert would be arriving with the Chairman of the Board the day after, to help resolve the explosive situation at hand. During the following days, Mr John Ford proved to be the voice of reason, able to get the labor union to the negotiating table to find a constructive and peaceful resolution for the future of the company and the employees.

When I moved to California in 1996, I immediately set about training to become a workplace mediator. I also obtained a certificate in Training and Human Resource Development, and worked hard to build a Workplace Conflict Management practice that included mediation, training, coaching and teaching.

In 2000, I was contracted by the Equal Employment Opportunity Commission to conduct mediations, and shortly thereafter was selected to serve on the United States Postal Service (USPS) workplace mediation program, called REDRESS.

These and other experiences mediating informal Equal Employment Opportunity (EEO) disputes for federal agencies in California have exposed me to the various ways conflicts are experienced, framed and resolved in the United States. It was apparent to me as I mediated many of these cases – both internally and externally – that opportunities had been missed early on, when the conflict was still internal to the organization. And so, I committed to keep 'swimming upstream' away from the courthouse, and to work on the early recognition and resolution of workplace conflict. This is consistent with my goal of helping HR managers to approach and resolve conflict with greater clarity and confidence through early recognition and resolution.

I continue to mediate for the USPS REDRESS mediation program and other federal agencies. For the most part, my practice now focuses on conflict internal to organizations. HR managers ask me to mediate disputes between employees, and also to work with teams who are struggling to deal productively with conflict. I am also often asked to mediate post-investigation or post-hearing.

In addition to corporate training that focuses on conflict resolution, I have taught extensively at local universities in the San Francisco Bay Area, including for a time in the Human Resource Management (HRM) Certificate Program at San Francisco State University. Currently, I teach negotiation to law students at UC Hastings, and mediation to business and psychology students at Golden Gate University. I also teach an online class on Organizational Collaboration three times a year to students at Creighton University, Omaha, Nebraska. For two years, I directed a graduate Organizational Conflict Management Certificate Program at John F. Kennedy University, and during that time conducted many 'in-house' mediations to help nip things in the bud. Here is what Teri Cannon, Dean of the School of Law at John F. Kennedy University, had to say:

> *John has handled several mediations involving students, faculty and staff. He is one of the most effective mediators I have worked with. He has a way of gaining the trust of the parties in a mediation setting and has a calming effect in even the most contentious of situations. He handles issues relating to diversity with skill and sensitivity. His ethics are above reproach, and his understanding of human nature is extraordinary. I always think of him first when I need a mediator.*

Since 2007, I have been the trainer of the Northern California Human Resources Association's two-day course on Mastering Workplace Mediation, and since 2013 the teacher of UC Berkeley Extension's class on Internal Workplace Mediation for the HR Professional. In many ways, the experience of training HR managers in the skill of mediation, and seeing how eager and ready they are to learn, has inspired me to write this book.

In 2010, I made a return to divorce mediation through Liaise Divorce Solutions LLC, a firm based in San Francisco. Founder David Stein's mission is to change the way Americans get divorced. Reframing family dissolution to marital reorganization using technology, including online video conferencing, makes this bold approach to mediation exciting, and also something I am proud to be a part of.

Along the way I have been President of the Association for Dispute Resolution of Northern California, and was the Managing Editor of Mediate.com from 2000 to 2011.

I wanted to share a few things about myself, and specifically about my experience in the field of conflict management, so that you could decide whether my experience qualifies me to talk about a practical tool that allows us to imagine and realize peace together. Each of you has a unique story that explains why you are reading this book. While the context and culture in which you practice may be different, I hope you will find the insights and approaches in this book transferable and of value to you.

Acknowledgements

When I was getting started in the United States, I went to Houston, Texas, to get certified by Daniel Dana as a trainer on his two one-day programs: Self Mediation and Managerial Mediation. I am deeply indebted to his insights regarding how to bring the skill of mediation into the workplace.

I am also indebted to Gregorio Billikopf's thinking on the challenge of workplace mediation, and am grateful for the clear expression of his ideas in his book *Party Directed Mediation*, especially regarding the importance of a pre-mediation meeting.

In terms of the fundamentals of mediation, I have relied heavily on two books: *The Mediation Process* by Christopher Moore and *Managing Public Disputes* by Susan Carpenter and William Kennedy. The latter book does an excellent job of distilling a simple process, which is the basis for the mediation structure that I use and have articulated in this book.

William Wilmot and Joyce Hocker's *Interpersonal Conflict* is an excellent text and a good backbone for the basics. These authors' emphasis on identity and relationship needs is significant. Another foundational text on which I have drawn extensively is Bernard Mayer's *The Dynamics of Conflict Resolution*. However, the foundational logic of the problem-solving process is sourced from *Getting to YES* by Roger Fisher, William Ury and Bruce Patton.

My thinking about conflict management draws on the work of Kenneth Cloke, author of *Mediating Dangerously*. And I have been inspired by my close friend, Eileen Barker, on the topic of forgiveness. Both are adept at literally getting to the heart of the matter, and are intuitive pioneers in knowing how best to work with emotions in conflict.

Similarly, both Cinnie Noble, author of *Conflict Management Coaching*, and Craig E. Runde, Director of the Center for Conflict Dynamics, were ever-present with me as I wrote this book. They both embody a deep knowing about what it takes to work with people in conflict.

I would also like to thank the founders of Mediate.com, Jim Melamed and John Helie, for believing in me and entrusting me to edit the article and blog content for their award-winning website for over ten years. The privilege of my position granted me a unique vantage point from which to observe the field of mediation in conversation with itself through the articles submitted. The ideas of the authors of these articles are everywhere in this book. Thank you all!

My thinking on the role of emotion in conflict is influenced by a score of writers, starting with Daniel Goleman, author of *Emotional Intelligence*, and neuroscientist Antonio Damasio. I am a big fan of John Gottman's evidence-based research into relational dynamics, and I join Professor Peter Coleman from my field of conflict management in calling for our own evidence-based research to back up and expand on our intuitive ways of knowing. His exciting new book, *The Five Percent*, shares some of the research that is currently being undertaken.

Malcolm Gladwell fascinated me in *Blink*, and, in his engaging manner, led me to the likes of Gottman, as well as to Paul Ekman. The latter is central to the modern view of emotions, especially as to how they are shown through facial expressions. Authors like Gladwell point to the ways in which we are far more emotional in our rationality than we ever suspected.

At a practical level, the ideas expressed in *Difficult Conversations* by Douglas Stone, Bruce Patton and Sheila Heen are excellent pointers as to how we integrate the various conversations in which the participants in a conflict are involved, whether it be about the facts, the feelings, or the assumptions made. Marshall Rosenberg's *Nonviolent Communication* has become the standard for 'I' statement technology, and I drew heavily on his work and insights, especially as to how we communicate our feelings.

When it comes to the practice of mediation, I am forever indebted to those who have given me an opportunity to mediate, train, teach, coach and consult with in conflict situations. You have been my most important teachers by allowing me to learn from experience. This includes all my clients and students, ever. Thank you!

As to the writing, editing and production of this book, these special friends and colleagues deserve a mention: Olga Africawala, Steve Ajay, Eileen Barker, Steffi Berkowitz, Marthe Dalton, Danika Davis, Beth Delaney, John Helie, Jim Melamed, Kathleen McCauley, Jane Mock, Kerri Moon, Cynthia Remmers, Colin Rule, Peta Scop, and Jerry Straks.

Thank you to my star editor, Avrille du Plessis, and to Perri Caplan for the proofreading, layout and indexing, and to Jane Sheppard for the cover design.

John Ford
Oakland, CA
2014

Chapter 1
Introduction

*"The talent most lacking in corporate America
is the ability to effectively manage
conflict in the workplace."*
Bob Delaney

I wrote this book specifically for HR managers who want to master the skill of mediation. It is very much a 'how to' book that seeks to demystify mediation and make it available to managers of people, like you.

Is this you?

The first assumption I make about you is that, for whatever reason, you are not afraid of *other people's* conflict. In fact, you are drawn to it in a strange way and are already approaching conflict situations with what I call the 'mediation stance'. This does not mean you are comfortable with *your own* conflict, or that you manage it well. However, you recognize that conflict is inevitable and that there is more to conflict resolution than fight and flight.

Secondly, you are frustrated by the way in which conflict is currently being handled in your organization. In particular, while you understand the need for efficient fact-finding procedures to establish whether a breach of law or policy has occurred, like compliance investigations and hearings, in your opinion this strategy is overplayed. You think that it is often used instead of what is actually needed, which is getting people to talk to each other. Even when the strategy is legitimately used to determine whether allegations are true or not, it often generates collateral relational damage and emotional fallout.

Thirdly, you have an innate ability to help others in conflict, and, importantly, you want to make a difference in order to make your organization more peaceful. You are aware of mediation as an approach to resolving organizational conflict, and you are eager to learn how to use it. Even if you are unsure about your natural ability to mediate, you consider conflict resolution and mediation a skill set that can be learnt. My belief is that this is precisely why you are reading this book. While it is true that many mediators have innate skills, like leadership, mediation is indeed a skill set that can be learnt.

Goals of this book

My goal is to support you to successfully master the skill of workplace mediation. I want to make it easy for you to gain confidence in your ability to mediate. I want to share with you what I have learnt from working as a professional mediator with an employment and workplace focus. I am going to reveal all I know about resolving conflict as easily as possible, so that you can do it too.

I am also going to weave in what I have learnt academically while teaching graduate students the skills of conflict resolution, negotiation and mediation. For some time now, as part of my corporate training practice, I have taught HR managers the skill of mediation through the offices of the Northern California Human Resources Association. Although a book can never replace the learning that occurs in a classic training environment, my hope is to convey to you, through these pages, what I cover when training your colleagues.

I do not have to tell you how debilitating poorly managed workplace conflict can be. It can be especially difficult when you are directly involved in the conflict, but also when you experience conflict indirectly through your HR role. I want to give you the tools to do something productive about it.

Conflict does not have to be a headache. In fact, it should be seen as a sign of vitality; a sign that something needs to change within an organization. Having mediation as a tool can go a long way to support authentic organizational harmony and well-being. And if you are the one doing the mediation, you get the accolades for being a peacemaker!

Mediation defined

Mediation is a conciliatory process in which an acceptable third party intervenes in the conflict or disputes of participants, in our case, employees, with the goal of supporting them to reach agreement.

This definition of mediation is given close attention in Chapter 5.

Mediation is a process that is premised on the belief that involving a third party in a conflict can be helpful. The goal of the mediator is to intervene in a manner that supports participant self-determination. This means that the mediator is not the decision maker. Our role is to *not* make decisions. The participants in our mediations are always the ones who are responsible for what happens. We facilitate their conversations and negotiations, and support them as they make their own decisions. If we make the decisions, whether directly or in effect through the application of too much pressure, we move out of our mediator role.

For those who harbor a lingering confusion about the distinction between mediation and arbitration, decision-making responsibility is at the heart of the distinction. Arbitrators engage in a fact-finding process and decide who wins and who loses. They make the decisions for the disputants. Mediators are facilitators who *do not* decide. And while we often think of both mediation and arbitration as formal processes that are conducted by 'professionals', we can also say that managers both mediate and arbitrate, depending on who is responsible for any decisions.

Who can mediate?

In most parts of the world, mediation is unregulated, and when it is regulated, this normally occurs in the formal legal context. This means that you do not need permission to mediate within your organization, and you are not required to take any mediation training (although training is recommended). What matters most is whether you are *acceptable* to the disputants who are in conflict. It also means that you are not the only one who can mediate. Any employee can mediate. In most organizations, there are the peacemakers – those employees towards whom others naturally gravitate because of their ability to help when there is a conflict.

Some organizations train cadres of employees to be available to provide workplace mediations. Other organizations train their managers to be managerial mediators and to adopt a mediation stance as much as possible. Increasingly, Employee Relations (ER) specialists are trained to conduct mediations. And, of course, there are the external professional mediators who are available to come in and help out.

Why mediation makes sense

For those who need convincing, I offer some reasons to mediate.

Firstly, it saves money. In 2010, the RAND Institute for Civil Justice estimated that it cost, on average, $150,000 to defend an employment discrimination lawsuit in the United States. But the costs of poorly managed conflict are not limited to the legal costs that are incurred when your organization has to defend itself in court. When a conflict drags on and on, and ensnares more and more bystanders, the amount of time spent is staggering. To find out just how staggering, estimate the time spent by each individual employee affected by the conflict, and then multiply this time by each person's salary!

Add to this the indirect costs of absenteeism, staff turnover, restructuring of the workflow to accommodate conflicts, health costs, theft and sabotage, and – not unimportantly – lower productivity, and you will begin to get to the real cost of poorly managed conflict. The bottom line is that conflict costs money, and for the most part, unless it shows up as legal fees, that cost is not being measured.

A second reason to use mediation is a practical one. HR managers need a variety of tools to get their job done. Mediation is one such tool. It should not replace the fact-finding investigation or hearing, but it needs to be added to the HR toolbox. Investigations are required to determine whether there has been a law or policy violation and what to do about it. Mediations are required to resolve conflict, especially when an important ongoing relationship is in trouble.

Beyond cost savings and pragmatism, there are myriad other good reasons to consider mediation in your organization. Mediation as a process has a lot of integrity. It values self-determination, is respectful of the need for privacy and confidentiality, and promotes voluntary participation. This means that participants in a mediation have high levels of control in a safe process.

Although success is never guaranteed, mediation results in a mutually acceptable resolution most of the time (in over eighty percent of cases). Mediation is therefore hopeful and helps to chart a better future. It increases the possibility of lasting peace through sincere reconciliation.

Conflict is a call to explore ourselves, including our levels of self-awareness or consciousness, and our emotional maturity. Mediation often creates the space for profound insights which frequently lead to shifts in perception, learning and growth.

And, if HR managers assume a mediation stance and support both their managers and their employees to work out their own conflicts, without taking sides, they avoid the perception that HR is simply a biased arm of management.

Finally, mediation can be used to resolve a wide range of situations. As an early intervention, it can be effective to address trust and identity issues in relationships before a conflict spins out of control. At the other extreme, as the legal profession has found, mediation can be used effectively to resolve employment lawsuits that have turned workplaces into veritable war zones.

When to mediate

Attending to conflict early on is always a good idea. Waiting for destructive behaviors or for a formal dispute to emerge means that we have missed early opportunities to nip the conflict in the bud. As an HR manager, you should do your best to be alert to the earlier but more subtle warning signs that tell you conflict is brewing. Yet you cannot be everywhere, and the truth is that you are not responsible for your line management's conflicts. As a result, you will become aware of many conflicts only after much water has flowed under the bridge, often by noticing signs of intense struggle, polarization and escalation. When you do become aware of these conflicts, you will be able to use the skills you have learnt in this book to support the emergence of a successful resolution to these acute and sometimes chronic conflicts.

Of course, if your organization has to investigate a workplace complaint as a matter of law or policy, you may consider using mediation in conjunction with the investigation or, as is becoming more popular, after the investigation. This can be especially helpful where either one or both of the employees involved are unhappy with the fact of the investigation and/or the outcome, and still need to work together.

Some conflicts are not resolved and end up in the administrative or legal system as a result of formal complaints filed by your employees. Although at this point your role is more likely to be that of an organizational representative, in most jurisdictions there will be further options for mediation. This is certainly true in California, where both the state Department of Fair Employment and Housing and the federal Equal Employment Opportunity Commission have mediation programs. In addition, most state and federal courts will encourage the use of mediation before going to trial for employment and labor matters.

Suitability of mediation

Generally, mediation is a great idea where there is an ongoing relationship that is characterized by poor communication and emotional charge, the so-called personality conflicts. Employees are too often transferred or moved, at great expense and inconvenience to the organization, in order to accommodate an ongoing personality conflict. Although transferring an employee may be the best solution in some cases, employees should be expected to address their interpersonal conflict directly, and be supported through a process like mediation, if necessary.

To be able to participate in mediation, the parties need to be able to listen to one another, communicate their needs, and negotiate. Where a participant is too upset or extremely hostile, mediation may not work. However, this is often more a question of timing, and one of the strengths of mediation is its ability to address strong emotions.

The reality is that you usually meet your mediation participants at the place where they are on their life path, especially as regards emotional self-awareness and personal responsibility. It can be very difficult mediating with emotionally immature individuals who assume a victim mentality and are fixated on vindication. That said, you may choose to mediate notwithstanding the immaturity of one or more of the participants. This is because an agreement or a narrowing of the issues is still going to be better than a chronic unresolved conflict situation.

It is not unusual for the underlying or real issues not to be addressed during the resolution of a formal complaint. For example, an employee alleges discriminatory intent in relation to the way vacations are assigned. An investigation establishes that there is no bias, and so while the formal complaint may have been resolved from the organization's perspective, the underlying tension between the manager making the assignments and the employee has not. In this case, mediation would be the perfect tool to help explore what is going on and to help restore the productive relationship between the employee and manager through creative solutions.

Mediation may not be appropriate when an employer wants to establish a precedent to create certainty about a policy. In those rare situations, an employer may need an administrative agency, court or arbitrator to rule on the issue at hand.

Organization of this book

I want to make it easy for you to learn the skill of mediation. However, you are going to have to do more than just read this book. You need to practice and acquire hands-on experience. For an HR manager, gaining experience should be easy, especially as you start noticing how often the basic elements of mediation are at play: you (the third-party HR manager) supporting two employees to find their own solutions.

I have included some useful resources at the end of the book that should help you to get started and to sustain you along the way. There is a sample agreement to mediate, an opening statement, and – importantly – a 'laundry list' of typical agreement clauses that you will be able to use in the mediations you conduct.

I explore the mindset of the mediator through the postures of the mediator's stance in Chapter 2, and then conflict resolution (Chapter 3) and the key communication skills of the mediator (Chapter 4). In Chapter 5, I review my definition of mediation in detail, and in the ensuing chapters consider the various phases of mediation, from the room set up and opening statement in Chapter 6, to the education phase (Chapter 7), the option-generation phase (Chapter 8), the negotiation phase (Chapter 9) and, finally, the closing phase (Chapter 10). In Chapter 11, I take a closer look at both the structured caucus and the importance of follow-up. In Chapter 12, I apply the lessons learnt to the fictitious situation Harry and Sally are facing, and see how mediation could work for them. Chapter 13 concludes by looking to the future.

Chapter 2
The Mediator's Stance

*"The various elements of posture are
combined together in the qi gong stance."*
Kenneth S. Cohen

In martial arts training, students are taught the benefit of various body and mental postures. The totality of these postures, when adopted together, amounts to an effective stance for defense and attack. Students are taught to adopt this stance when presented with a challenge, notwithstanding any contrary reflexive or reactive instincts or habits. The familiarity of the stance inspires confidence and prepares them to meet their reality with competence and agility. It ensures that they are on the best footing possible.

In mediation, there are a number of key postures that are helpful to adopt, that together can be described as the mediator's stance. In essence, the stance is more of an attitude and mindset which ensures that you do no harm, while supporting collaboration and the emergence of a creative solution. It prepares you to respond consciously in the moment when mediating, and allows you to mediate informally.

Supporting the resolution of conflict through mediation is considered a high-level emotional intelligence skill that integrates and draws on all the domains of emotional intelligence: self-awareness, self-management, social awareness, and relationship management.[1] As I review the mediator's stance in this chapter, what will become apparent is how important it is for you as the mediator to be self-aware, not only of your emotional footprint but also of the thought patterns that both enable and limit your ability to mediate.

The ability to consciously adopt the mediator's stance, especially in the chaos of conflict, requires a calm mind and a relaxed body. You need to be able to access the wisdom of your intuition.

In mediation, you need to connect with and attune to the conflicted participants. This requires good people skills, to maintain and foster harmony without taking sides. It is this sense of connection that enables you to stay in touch with what is going on, to read the currents, pick up the vibe, and intervene in ways that promote collaboration. What matters ultimately as a mediator is how you guide the conflicted participants in an emotionally resonant manner towards the possibility of a resolution without doing any harm or making decisions for them.

Let us take a closer look at the different elements of the mediator's stance:

1. The real self
2. Relaxed and calm
3. Open to subtle information and feedback
4. Empathic rapport builder
5. Balanced and omnipartial: equally there for everyone
6. Collaborative process guide, not decision maker
7. Keeper of confidences
8. Respecter of differences
9. Inspiring beacon of hope

1. The real self

"When we present ourselves to the world without a mask and keep it real, we offer the same opportunity for others to do the same."
Madisyn Taylor

Shakespeare's call to be true to ourselves in Hamlet is easier said than done, mainly because of the challenge of knowing ourselves. If we do not know ourselves, how can we be true to ourselves? And, as if that were not enough, the concept of 'self' is contested in society.

We often think of ourselves as our social identity and the voice in our head. While our ego plays a vital role in our ability to engage meaningfully in the external world, the danger is that we mistake this one aspect of ourselves for the whole. Beyond our ego and all the helpful roles it can play, there is an unchanging aspect of ourselves that is conscious as an observer and a deeper guide to our lives. In my opinion, this fundamental consciousness is the real self, and when you are able to act from this place, you will find the firm ground of authenticity.

What is important is that you consider your concept of self and be as true to that as you can be. Ultimately, the best person you can be is you. For the real (not false) self to be present in this way requires self-knowledge of who you are *and* who you are not.

If you do not know yourself, you are more likely to want to hide behind a mask. You may become defensive, pretend to know things you do not know, and try to create the impression that you have abilities that you do not have. However, when you act authentically (from the place of real self), you are transparent, and encourage the participants in the mediation to be real with one another.

You also need to play different egoic roles without attaching to any. Some years ago, the American Arbitration Association identified some of the roles a mediator plays, which include being the facilitator, scapegoat, trainer, agent of reality, resource expander, and problem solver. Authenticity is maintained in the knowing that you are your real self and not the roles that you play.

You need the courage to act in alignment with your deepest sense of self as revealed by your values, and not hide behind any masks or roles. When you are clear about your values, they guide you. When you know yourself, you can act in ways that are true to yourself when presented with challenging situations. You know what you will and will not do; that 'yes' means yes and 'no' means no. It is this knowing that allows you to act with integrity and be of true service to others.

Consistently applying your values is the hallmark of integrity. To do this, you need to take the time to explore your deepest beliefs about the world as you compassionately examine and address the question of who you really are. As mediators, this knowing ourselves includes a consideration of a relevant set of ethical standards of conduct, which are usually determined by the milieu in which we live. Most embody common sense guidelines on matters that are central to being a mediator, such as self-determination, confidentiality and neutrality. At the very least, you should review the standards of conduct for mediators in order to determine your own.

2. Relaxed and calm

"Stay calm and relaxed, as if nothing in the world bothers you!"
Unknown

When we are relaxed, we are at ease and without unnecessary tension in our body. When we are calm, we are not worried or bothered and can be at peace with what is unfolding. We are like the calm eye in the center of a storm. When we are relaxed in our body and calm in our mind, we are able to be present in the moment and respond at our natural best.

Remaining relaxed and calm is not easy, especially when attempting to mediate. At a practical level, mediators need to monitor their internal state. If something is disturbing you, you are not relaxed and calm. Understanding what is bothering you, and being able to restore a calm and relaxed state within you, is vital for yourself and the participants in the mediation.

Most behavioral patterns that signal an emotional disturbance fall into one of two protective strategies. The first is when we behave in a volatile way. We battle the danger of eruptions when our amygdala shuts down our ability to be restrained and sensitive. We then display anger and act upon it. The second strategy, typically more fear based, is when we suppress our emotionality, sometimes consciously but mostly unconsciously. The risk with this strategy is the random leakage of emotions and the display of passive-aggressive behavior.

As mediators, we need to model being real with our emotionality, and to respond consciously rather than react unconsciously. We therefore need to know what triggers us and how we react at our worst. We also need to develop effective strategies to manage our own unruly emotions. The practice of breathing as a primary calming tool cannot be overemphasized. I encourage a few deep breaths before every mediation. When I notice I am bothered by something during a mediation, I find deep breathing an excellent tool to restore my relaxed and calm state. I can then connect and respond consciously to what is actually unfolding in the moment.

3. Open to subtle information and feedback

"The quieter you become, the more you are able to hear."
Rumi

When you are mediating, you are constantly presented with the dilemma of what to do next. Your choice, whatever it may be, is dependent on your openness to feedback. Instead of following a rigid plan, you need to meet your reality and respond with an intervention that is sensitive to the participants' needs in the moment.

Once you have acted authentically, with what you believe to be the wisest intervention, you should eagerly anticipate the next round of feedback. If your intervention is having the desired effect, great! If not, you need to act on the new feedback and do something different. This is the heart of the work.

Intuition

How we resolve the dilemma of what to do next, based on the feedback we have received, brings us to the most subtle form of sensing used by mediators – sensing things intuitively. Intuition is that sense of knowing without knowing why. Unlike conscious thought, where we apply theory to facts, intuition is sourced from the unconscious. Without being fully aware of the underlying reasons or theory, we have a spontaneous sense of knowing. This emerges primarily as a feeling, an image, a hunch, or a sense that we consider strong enough to act upon.

How, then, do we develop our intuition? In her classic book, *Awakening Intuition*, Frances Vaughan offers an approach that allows our whole being to be a more receptive sensor to what is going on.[2] She suggests that we quieten our minds, both before and during situations where we need our intuition.

Vaughan encourages an open sensitivity to subtle information in the form of feelings and images as the primary way to get in touch with our intuition. She warns that if we have not cleansed our own emotional bodies – our projections, transference and triggers – we will be distracted from picking up the subtle messages that are being sent. She points to meditation as a key tool that allows intuition to come into conscious awareness without interference.

To receive intuitive information, we need to be relaxed and calm in order to discern the difference between the noise of our egoic mind and sensed insight and wisdom that is available when we are quiet and acting from the place of real self. As we continue to discover the value of our bodies as sources of information about what is going on emotionally, we gain confidence in our ability to sense what it is we are feeling at a visceral level, and notice more of what our 'gut' is telling us. We listen in the silence and trust the information that comes to our attention.

Facial expressions

Body language is another source of information that can be especially helpful to sense the emotional energy at play. It is a rich source of information for mediators, and includes the display of emotions through both facial expressions and body gestures.

As an observer of emotional expressions, try not to second guess people or catch them out. Rather, establish baseline expressions and gestures early on so that you can notice deviations from the norm. Then pay attention to these deviations, as well as other subtle expressions of emotions, at moments when sensitive or difficult information is being shared.

Psychiatrist Paul Ekman at the University of California, San Francisco (UCSF), established that facial expressions are universal and that we are all born hardwired to express a wide range of affective states.[3] Because of the ancient circuitry, these expressions provide reliable information about what is actually going on emotionally, rather than what is being masked. Whether one is an Inuit, an African or an American, a smile is a smile. Anger is anger. And unless we are actors, these emotions are difficult to fake. Ekman identifies seven core emotions – fear, disgust, anger, sadness, surprise, happiness and contempt. He also describes with great precision the exact musculature that is engaged for each of them.

It is a good idea to learn to recognize emotions by interpreting facial expressions with confidence. Ekman has developed online learning materials that help you to develop this skill. You will learn that with anger, there is a tightening of the lips and a furrowing of the brow. With sadness, the eyebrows join high and there may be a wobble on the chin. A one-sided smile, often called a smirk, shows contempt. A smile can be genuine or social – the former involves the contraction of the muscles around the eyes and accounts for the twinkle that politeness does not bring. Fear is sometimes confused with surprise because the eyes are open with both, but fearful eyes are less round, and there is more of a glare. With fear, the mouth has an almost triangular shape and pulls down. Disgust shows in the center line as a scrunching upward of the face, and is often confused with anger.

Gestures

Beyond the facial expressions are the gestures of the body. They are easier to mask precisely because they are controlled by a part of the brain that allows for voluntary direction. Gestures are therefore less reliable indicators of emotions. For example, it is easier to learn not to cover your mouth with your hand when you lie than not to display, even fleetingly as a microexpression that you quickly mask, the moment when you are genuinely surprised.

In addition, where facial expressions are fairly universal, gestures can be culturally specific. For instance, a thumbs-up gesture does not mean the same thing everywhere. We should therefore proceed with caution as we pay attention to gestures.

There are some gestures that are so grand that they are hard to ignore. The hands and feet are especially expressive. Hand-to-head movements are interesting displays of distress, especially if synonymous with a difficult question. They can point to deception or, at the very least, fear. When it comes to the feet, try to watch for curling toes as a sign of discomfort. Digging in of the toes is usually a sign of determination.

Remember to be cautious and open to the possibility that you may have misinterpreted a gesture.

Tone

We have considered non-verbal information that we gain through what we see (facial expressions and body gestures). Tone provides emotional information through what we hear.

In his book *Blink*, Malcolm Gladwell explores the fascinating studies that were conducted to see why some surgeons were being sued while others were not.[4] What is interesting is that it is not quality of care but good communication that is the determinant. An initial study by Levinson recorded interviews of these surgeons with their patients.[5] She found that those who were not sued had spent, on average, three minutes longer with their patients. They had also listened well and had used orienting comments and appropriate humor.

In a follow-up study by Ambady, 40-second clips from the original Levinson study were content-filtered to retain intonation, pitch and rhythm but erase content (the actual words used).[6] Ambady asked laypeople to review the clips, and based on what they heard, determine which surgeons had been sued. With this very limited information (mainly intonation), participants were able to make accurate predictions. Surgeons who had been sued had used a dominant tone, while those who had not often sounded anxious. Ambady concluded that a dominant tone is interpreted as a sign of not caring, while an anxious tone is interpreted as showing concern.

Clearly, the old saying is correct – it is not what you say, but how you say it. As mediators, we need to pay careful attention to intonation as a vital source of information about emotionality.

Feedback

Ideally, you should use all your experiences as the grist for your learning mill. You need to be aware of the relationship between your self-awareness and your ability to be of service as a mediator. When you are given feedback, accept it as a gift. If it is painful, try not to react defensively by thinking of all the reasons the person is wrong. Rather, seek the grain of truth in what is being said.

4. Empathic rapport builder

"The best way to persuade people is with your ears – by listening to them."
Dean Rusk

Nothing can be a substitute for the rapport the mediator establishes with each of the participants in the mediation. In everything you do, seek to build trust and confidence (rapport) between yourself and the participants. Ultimately, rapport reveals your degree of influence and allows you to guide the participants towards resolution.

Trust

"He who does not trust enough will not be trusted."
Lao Tze

Trust is the knowledge that we can rely on another to care about our goodwill and interests. Trust is hard earned, takes time to grow, and can be eroded quickly. Some mediators imagine they have opened a trust account with each participant. They seek to build as much trust as possible so that they can make withdrawals when, at certain times in the mediation, they need to say something difficult, such as asking a participant a sensitive question.

Participants often have significant blind spots. Whether and how we address them takes trust and a delicate touch.

So, how do we build trust? It starts the minute we start interacting. We are cordial and friendly. We greet, say thank you, and goodbye. We make eye contact and we smile. We also listen empathically so that everyone feels heard and understood. This is probably the most important skill that all mediators acknowledge as vital to building trust.

Mediators are reliable. We do what we say we will do when we say we will do it. We keep confidences, and communicate with care and sensitivity. We are tactful. We clarify our role as mediator. We are clear about how we support the emergence of an agreement. We know what we will do, and also what we will not do. We model respectful communication. We are not afraid to be real and authentic, despite the risk of possible harmful consequences.

Most fundamentally, mediators build the caring aspect of trust through vulnerability. When people share what is going on, they become vulnerable and take the risk that what they share may be used against them in the future. If this risk is not realized, then trust grows, but if it is realized, trust is eroded. It is that simple! That is why empathic listening is so powerful. If you are able to connect through an empathic listening posture, and safely reward the vulnerable expression through validation, then trust grows.

Confidence

"With confidence, you can reach truly amazing heights; without confidence, even the simplest accomplishments are beyond your grasp."
Marianne Williamson

As mediators, we need to be confident in our abilities. Like a mountain guide who realistically says, yes we can get to the top, we say, yes we can get to yes. We can get to resolution. We are the beacon of hope. It is about knowing and believing in our ability. Confidence is related to competence. And, like trust, competence in a new skill takes time to develop. So we take baby steps, and with each step our competence and confidence grows. Our growing confidence will be felt in the open emotional system and have a beneficial effect on the mediation process.

We also need to conduct the mediation process in a way that allows the participants to grow their confidence in their ability to resolve the conflict through the carefully measured steps of the mediation process. Signing an agreement to mediate is a baby step that builds confidence. Reaching agreements on ground rules is another step that has the same impact.

When the participants see that you are prepared, it inspires confidence in your ability. Appearing ready is a good thing. However, the goal of preparation is not to predetermine and control, but to give you the necessary agility to respond to the reality you meet. If things are different, you need to respond to that, not to the reality you imagined during your preparation. If you spend too much time thinking about what you are going to do next, or worrying about what you just did, you will miss what is going on in the moment.

5. Balanced and omnipartial: equally there for everyone

"Do you want to know what my secret is? I don't mind what happens."
Krishnamurti

Our experience of riding a bicycle provides an interesting window into balance. As you know, you push down hard on the right pedal and follow with an equally hard push on the left. Once you start moving and you gain momentum, it is easy to balance and you do not have to pedal that hard.

Balance in mediation is similar. You listen empathically to the one participant, and then to the other. When you are listening to the one, it is like you are pushing down on the right side. Then, when you are listening to the other, you are pushing down on the left. You strive for balance in the momentum that emerges. And then you are listening to both. The momentum grows and you move forward.

Balance is the essence of the mediation stance. A mediator does not take sides. Our intention is to be there for all, and to be fair and balanced in all that we do. To this extent, it can be said that mediators are omnipartial.

In real life, however, it is seldom possible to be perfectly balanced. That is why the best we can do is to show that we are working hard to realize our intention to be there for all. That is the crucial perceptual piece. Whether or not we are succeeding in maintaining balance is for the participants to decide.

When you take the side of management, you are not adopting the mediation stance and you are making it difficult for yourself. When you adopt the mediation stance, you are being there for both the manager and the employee. You hold the space for them to address their concerns directly, with your balanced help, if needs be.

The participants should decide whether we are acceptable as mediators. We should be willing to disclose potential conflicts of interest of relevance to the mediation. And if we are no longer acceptable, we should withdraw. Remember, the mediator is there in the service of the participants.

6. Collaborative process guide, not decision maker

"When one is to succeed in leading a person to a certain place, one must above all take care to find out where he is and start there."
Søren Kierkegaard

Being balanced or neutral about the substance of the matter does not mean that you do not care or support the process. Mediators are like mountain guides who use experience and innate knowledge of the mountain to support the mountaineers to accomplish their goals. Mediators guide the process of conflict resolution, communication, negotiation, and forgiveness.

As we guide and interact with the interplay between the participants, we observe both the collaborative and the competitive moments. We should not rescue either participant from the conflict, but constantly seek to reframe towards collaboration. It is in this regard that we are not balanced. We need to lean the process towards collaboration as we guide. That is part of our stance.

Most conflict involves poor communication. To collaborate, we need to communicate; in fact, all we have is communication when it comes to resolving conflict. As mediators, we should model effective communication. We should strive to be powerful empathic listeners who communicate with clarity and frame things in a collaborative manner. Most mediators agree that active listening is central to the success of mediation. It is like a salve that always makes things better. We need to support effective communication during all negotiations, and help participants to deal with power imbalances in explicit ways.

In mediation, we need to be clear about our relationship to decision making. Our role is to *not* decide. The participants are responsible for making the decisions. You can talk about the decisions, and the potential for both good and bad outcomes as a result of them, but you should always stop short of making the decisions, whether in fact or by the application of undue pressure. Your duty as a guide is done when you know the participants have the information necessary to make an informed decision, in accordance with their needs and beliefs. The fact that you would do something differently does not matter. Mediation is based on participant self-determination.

7. Keeper of confidences

"If we give away another's private information (whether or not they find out), we also undermine our relationship with them, destroying trust and thereby degrading the integrity of the relationship."
Victoria Walton

Martti Ahtisari, former Finnish President and Nobel Peace Prize winner, is a well-known mediator. He once commented that the greatest compliment he was ever paid was when an Ethiopian participant expressed appreciation for the tactful way in which he was able to say difficult things to people that they did not want to hear.

As mediators, we need that kind of sensitivity. We need to be politically savvy and not put our foot in it. When asked to keep confidences, we should keep them. We are honored guests in the intimate lives of the participants with whom we work. Conflict is personal and usually reveals our private lives. We need to support the process of conflict resolution and take seriously the trust and confidence the participants place in us.

Establishing the extent to which confidences will be kept is an important task for the mediator. It puts the participants at ease and encourages them to be candid with one another. The basic logic is that to address and resolve a conflict, you need to share your perspective openly. This means saying how you feel, what you think, and what your needs are in order to move forward. If the participants are afraid that the information they share will be used against them, they will not want to share it.

In a workplace context, legal confidentiality is less relevant. However, the way in which what is said and agreed upon during the mediation is shared with other members of the organization is naturally of concern. Typically, the manager to whom the two conflicted employees report will want to see the terms of any settlement agreement. This is safer because it controls, through agreement, what information is shared with whom.

A practical aspect of confidentiality pertains to including identified confidants with whom the participants will probably discuss the mediation. Co-workers, spouses, partners, mentors, and friends are often aware of the mediation and will ask about it. By including these confidants in the confidentiality of the mediation, we acknowledge the reality that this communication occurs, and therefore build trust.

The City of Las Vegas, Nevada, recently promoted itself with a series of advertisements that ended with the catchphrase: "What happens in Las Vegas stays in Las Vegas." This conveys the essence of confidentiality. It is effective because it uses humor to ease the tension around the issue of confidentiality. The goal in mediation is to create a safe environment in which information can be shared without fear of negative consequences.

The expectation that confidences shared during the mediation will be privileged from disclosure is typically achieved through a written agreement between the participants and the mediator. These agreements are either provided by external professional mediators or through policy documents associated with an internal mediation program. They define the scope and limitations of the confidentiality agreed upon. A sample is included as Appendix 1 on page 159.

A common assumption made when a confidentiality agreement is signed is that all communications within the mediation will be confidential. Yet, even where laws have been passed to protect confidentiality, there are limitations. It is thus good practice for mediators to clearly indicate the limits of the confidentiality agreement. For example, child abuse, threats of imminent harm to others, and admissions of criminal activities are usually excluded from protection in confidentiality agreements.

In the workplace, it may be prudent to craft additional exceptions to the confidentiality agreement to cover unlawful employment activity, such as harassment. This may be important where internal mediators are used, for instance, when an organization is construed as having been put on notice to conduct a fact-finding investigation for purposes of harassment legislation. One way organizations address this issue is by establishing that raising a concern in mediation *does not* constitute notice, and that if an employee has such a concern, the normal reporting channels should be followed. Another way the issue is addressed is by using external mediators who are not full-time employees of the organization.

Mediation programs need to be monitored to evaluate their efficiency and success. Confidentiality rules should not preclude responsible, statistical monitoring and evaluation. After the mediation is over, it is normal practice to report whether or not a settlement has been reached. With the consent of the participants, the terms of any agreement are often reported to peers and supervisors on a need-to-know basis.

8. Respecter of differences

"Different people, like different communities, have different strengths, and the only thing that works is using our different strengths together."
/'Angn!ao/'Un

Mediators respect both the cultural and style differences that emerge and are at play during the mediation.

Most simply, culture can be defined as the way things are done within a particular group, whereas style can be defined as the way things are done by each individual within a group. When mediating in the workplace, we need to consider the various layers of culture that are present – that of the country in which the organization is located, the industry, and the specific organization. Additionally, we should take into account the culture of the different work groups and departments within the organization. Finally, we meet the individuals, each of whom has a unique style.

Differences at the group level are usually those of culture, whereas differences at the individual level could be those of culture and/or style. Whether we are dealing with group differences or individual differences, we should be respectful and act with sensitivity. We also need to allow the participants to resolve the issues that may arise between them due to differences of culture or style.

Let us consider a dispute that centers on different ways of doing something that is informed by cultural values. What if the expectation is that everyone shares openly how they are feeling, yet one of the participants comes from a cultural background where privacy and restraint regarding the public expression of feelings is the norm. What would you do in this situation? Some would suggest that the 'when in Rome' rule should apply, in other words, that the person from the differing cultural background should adapt. Yet, if that happens, the dominant culture is reinforced and the message is given out that difference is unwelcome.

Ideally, participants should be able to acknowledge and transcend their cultural and style differences, at the group and individual levels, in order to focus on a solution that meets the needs of all. And, when one is open, one understands that different approaches taken by people due to culture and/or style variations lead to a more robust solution that is sensitive to the situation.

There is as much diversity within a culture as there is between cultures. Thus, rather than thinking that we should use our cross-cultural communication skills when we communicate across different cultural groups, we should assume that all communications are essentially cross-cultural.

9. Inspiring beacon of hope

"In my work as a mediator I use hope every day to encourage organizations to work with people they have given up on, and to encourage people who have given up on organizations, professionals, and the system, to give them a chance. Much more often than not, hope works!"
Caryn Cridland

'Contagion' is the word Goleman uses to describe the infectious quality of emotions. We feel together, and, through the openness of our emotional system, are able to influence the emotional states of others. As the mediator, you probably have the most significant influence over the emotional climate during the mediation. The mediation experience will be impacted negatively if you are anxious, distracted or insecure, but positively if you are relaxed, calm and hopeful.

As long as you are there, you signal hope for the participants. Your goal is to be real in your enthusiasm. Even if you are seldom consciously acknowledged, you are a reassuring figure and are appreciated. Return this appreciation by reminding the participants that you believe in them and their ability to resolve the conflict. Tell them that, in your experience, when people follow the mediation process, they find ways of improving their situation and often resolve the conflict in a lasting manner. Inspire the participants to make the best possible decision in the most creative manner with the resources at their disposal.

---

[1]   Goleman, 2002.
[2]   Vaughan, 1979.
[3]   Ekman, 2003.
[4]   Gladwell, 2005.
[5]   Levinson, 1997: 553-559.
[6]   Ambady, 2002: 5-9.

Chapter 3
Conflict Resolution for Mediators

*"We need models that not only see emotions as the energy
behind the conflicts, but also recognize that they create the
context through which we experience conflict."*
Peter T. Coleman

As mediators, we need to be comfortable with our own conflict and that of other people. More than that, we need a good understanding of the significance of conflict, and how to work effectively with participants to support their conflict resolution process, whether through external negotiation or internal forgiveness. We should always remember that we are assisting *their* conflict resolution process, not our own.

Let us start with a simple definition that addresses conflict in the external world. We can say that conflict is a behavioral struggle between interdependent parties over needs and resources. This is how external manifestations of conflict are most commonly framed. However, this definition has obvious limitations. We have all witnessed the emotional intensity of our reactions to conflict and know that emotions, and how we interpret them through our feelings, are very much part of the conflict experience. They are the expressions of energy that provide us with vital information that helps us get to the heart of the matter, often through an internal focus, like forgiveness.

In conflict, we also need to carefully watch our thought process. Firstly, we should think about how we interpret our public emoting as feelings and moods. Secondly, we need to consider the validity of our perceptions of interference, or scarcity, or incompatibility, and the negative quality we tend to attribute to one another's motives. Thirdly, we should factor into our thinking the limitations of our memory, and the distortions that occur during the retrieval of memories.

External manifestations of conflict are best resolved using a needs-focused negotiation process. Although it is tempting to focus on people's behavior, to get to a lasting peace, mediators need to find ways of addressing the emotional energy that holds the conflict in place, whilst shifting the participants' perceptions of the conflict. Getting to this level of resolution is not easy or possible in all mediations. You can encourage the participants to get real with one another (as you role model through the mediator's stance – see Chapter 2), but not everyone is open to working on their underlying emotional dynamics.

Emotional energy

"When we close the door to our feelings, we close the door to the vital currents that energize and activate our thoughts and actions."
Gary Zukav

When something happens, whether it be something that is done – as in an action, word or thought – or something that is not done, the first way we know we have a conflict is emotionally. It seems that basic emotional neural circuitry intercepts information, even if just by milliseconds, and causes us to react. Afterwards, the more refined neural pathways of the neocortex review what is going on and give us a more nuanced interpretation through our feelings.

Emotions are both responses to what is happening in the external world and to what is being generated by our thoughts. They can be viewed as a form of energy that provides information about our relationship to both the external and internal dimensions. Emotions are expressed physically in the moment mainly through the autonomic nervous system, but also through the voluntary nervous system.

We emote physically. Ideally, we should not resist or hold on to sensations, but rather allow them and then let them go. We need to feel and consciously express our emotions in a socially appropriate manner and then move on. We should not stew about things and get ourselves into thought-driven moods; rather, we should seek the message that the emotion is trying to reveal. When we feel our emotions in the present moment, they leave no significant residue; when we carry them into the future, they form a residue. This unintegrated energy is often referred to as emotional baggage.

Sometimes, our emotions relate to what is happening in the moment and provide us with useful guidance as we make a decision. At other times, however, they relate to something that has happened in the past. In this case, unresolved emotional energy is stimulated by an external event and seeks release through being felt. Making the mental connection to the actual source of our emotions, and then letting ourselves emote, allows the necessary release of energy.

When we allow people to feel what they are emoting, especially to feel what they had resisted feeling when they originally emoted, they can change. This is at the heart of Gestalt therapy's theory of change.[1] It allows people to choose to resolve and move on. People can change when they are allowed to experience their feelings.

According to this simple idea, you allow yourself to feel now what you were not able to feel at an earlier time. When this happens, you slowly reduce the negative emotional charge in your body and are less likely to be triggered in the present moment. Deepak Chopra explains it thus:

> Until you make peace with negative feelings, they will persist. The way to deal with negativity is to acknowledge it. Nothing more is needed... Feel the feeling, whether it's anger, fear, envy, aggression, or anything else, and say, 'I see you. You belong to me.'[2]

This speaks to the potential of mediation, where profound insights are generated and healing occurs. Mediators need to be aware of the transformative potential that exists when the participants start to look at the energetic relationship between what is triggering them in the present moment, and the original emotional imprinting.

This also alerts us to the reality that until the participants experience an insight into the relationship between some past hurt and the way they are responding in the moment, they will project their emotional baggage, and blame one another. Each will focus on the other as being the causal point of the conflict when, in truth, the energetic causal point resides within both of them.

While it is true that certain emotions show up more often than others in conflict situations, all of the seven core emotional states identified by Paul Ekman – fear, disgust, anger, sadness, surprise, happiness, contempt (see Chapter 2) – are present at different times and to differing degrees of intensity. Although we may categorize emotions as either negative or positive, all emotions convey information that can guide decision making.

Thought processes

"It is hard to change our point of view in a conflict. Most often, it is because we are not nearly as interested in resolving the conflict and possibly creating a new 'pearl' as we are in being right."
Thomas Crum

We only consciously process a very small amount of the sensory information that our brain receives. This is because our conscious brain receives the information only after the more primitive emotional brain has filtered it. Furthermore, what we receive is colored by our emotions and is subject to an array of unconscious interpretative lenses (cognitive biases) that influence our decisions. In the context of conflict, we assume that there is not enough to go around. We perceive interference and conclude that our needs are incompatible with those of the person with whom we are in conflict.

Our perception of scarcity can be traced to the fact that we are loss averse. This means we feel the pain of loss more than we feel the pleasure of gain. When losses are at stake (for example, when we are on the line to pay for something), we are risk taking. When it appears that we may gain from a situation, we are fearful and often opt for that which is more secure. For the most part, we are unaware of these influences.

Not only are we loss averse, but we are constantly monitoring for fairness. When our expectations do not align with reality, we often respond in anger and reciprocate negatively. Our sense that the 'other' is interfering and that our respective goals are incompatible arises from a variety of biases that distort our perception.

The first is the fundamental error of attribution, which refers to the way we tend to give ourselves the benefit of the doubt and hold the world to a higher standard. We are often forgiving of our own mistakes, which we attribute to environmental factors beyond our control, but tend to be less forgiving of the mistakes of others, which we attribute to character defects.

Secondly, we tend to devalue gestures or offers made by others. We are primed to be wary. Also, we tend to be overconfident about things, then see our probable success through rose-tinted filters, should the matter escalate. Readjusting our perception of the probabilities of a particular outcome is not easy, yet often necessary.

Thirdly, we usually favor information that confirms our beliefs. This, known as confirmation bias, ensures that we are good at discounting information that does not fit our template of what has happened. We focus on that which supports us, and have a very hard time looking at dissenting information. We tend to think that we are right and others are wrong. This is why one of the key roles of the mediator is as the tactful agent of reality.

As mediators, we seek to inspire the participants to see the futility of confirmation bias, to go beyond right and wrong, and to embrace the complexity of life. We want them to meet in the field which Rumi describes as "beyond ideas of wrongdoing and right-doing". (Rumi famously said: "Out beyond ideas of wrongdoing and right-doing, there is a field. I'll meet you there.")

Mediators cannot change the way humans are hardwired to have certain cognitive biases. We can, however, bring awareness and our conscious attention to bear to guide the participants towards making informed decisions. We need to look for opportunities to explore the role of cognitive biases, as and when they come up in a conflict. It helps to let the participants know how ingrained our cognitive biases are, through normalizing. It also helps to tell them that we all share this challenge (this is called 'mutualizing').

After received information has been filtered by our cognitive biases, we start adding meaning based on our personal and cultural experiences. In a word, we make assumptions. We do this about all manner of things, but especially about motive. In the context of conflict, we typically impute a negative intention to each other's motives when we experience a painful impact.

Even though people are seldom purposively mean or unkind, we are usually quick to take offence. Stephen Covey is a proponent of the

90:10 principle, which is the idea that we control what happens in life only ninety percent of the time.[3] As some people say, offence is ten percent given and ninety percent taken.

When we do not take responsibility for our responses, we often end up describing ourselves as victims in some unfair situation that should be stopped. We tend to conclude that our 'opponent' is on a mission to interfere with our happiness, as is apparent from the way that person is obstructing the meeting of our legitimate needs. Not only that, as our perception tends to be of scarcity rather than of abundance, we believe that if we do not reinforce the protective reaction that our emotions have kickstarted, we will be taken advantage of.

This is where we, as mediators, often meet the participants. We find they often have strongly entrenched beliefs about the way things are. We need to help them to look at what is going on, and invite new interpretations of the same situation. This is not easy and should be done with care. We therefore need to be painstaking in our attention to building trust, and work hard to make sure that our impact is always positive and supportive of collaboration. Sometimes, the participants are able to change or shift their perception of the situation. When that happens, resolution usually follows. At other times, they are unable to see things differently. Yet, with careful guidance, they can still discover that it is in their best interests to work something out.

Fortunately, mediation is not a fact-finding process, like an investigation. We need to remind the participants of that early on, and frequently throughout the mediation. They can agree to disagree. They can hold on to their interpretation of things, of what they see to be right and wrong, and they can decide not to change. However, agreements reached under these conditions will not last as well.

Memory

"The weakest ink is more powerful than the strongest memory."
Confucius

Another mental challenge we all face relates to memory. Not only do we select and interpret information based on unconscious biases and then make assumptions (especially about motive and right and wrong), but our capacity to accurately store and retrieve data is also subject to challenges.

We know from experience about the challenges of memory. We have all forgotten something, whether it was a person's name or what we went into the other room to fetch. We have all had frustrating tip-of-the-tongue moments, where we know the information is in our memory but are unable to retrieve it. And we have all remembered things in self-serving ways, later having to admit that we were wrong.

Humans have explicit and implicit memories. The former, sometimes called declarative memory, is what comes into play when participants consciously recall what they remember happening. Implicit memory pertains to the tasks we perform out of habit, including motor skills. Conscious attention is not required to perform these tasks.

Confucius understood the challenges of explicit memory long ago when he said: "The weakest ink is more powerful than the strongest memory." In other words, memory is not that reliable, and one should always write down the things of importance. This is the reason for the so-called 'paper trail' which managers keep when they are documenting performance issues. What one often observes in conflict is the futile arm wrestling of memory.

The first challenge is that of converting short-term memory into long-term memory. It is only when something makes it into our long-term memory that our brain rewires. Information that does not make it into our long-term memory is lost. It seems that the brain is designed to forget almost everything.

One way we appear to remember things is when we repeatedly focus our conscious attention on them. By diligent repetition, we ingrain the information into our long-term memory. The other way is when what happens has a striking emotional component, for instance, when we have post-traumatic stress syndrome. The memory of the trauma is seared into our brain whether we like it or not, and ensures that we are sensitized to recognize the warning signs in the future. This enables us to protect ourselves from danger.

The second challenge with memory retrieval is how we slowly re-remember things over time through the filters of our biases. This results in a version of reality which slowly morphs to support our personal self-serving 'truth' about a situation. What with cognitive biases, our penchant to make assumptions, and the limits of our memory, we have to be extremely careful with matters of the mind. It is true to say that we are mostly unaware of how we make sense of the world, and of how we make decisions.

Behavioral struggle

"If we manage conflict constructively, we harness its energy for creativity and development."
Kenneth Kaye

Our employee handbooks do not prescribe our feelings. But they do dictate to us how we should act. Most management efforts are behavioral at heart. You never get into trouble for seething inside, as long as you do not allow your anger to erupt into destructive behavior.

Conflict theorists have identified conflict styles or strategies that derive from our basic stress reactions: flight and fight, and tend and befriend. Whether we agree with the focus on styles as proposed by Kenneth Thomas and Ralph Kilmann,[4] or whether we agree with the strategies suggested by Alexander Hiam,[5] we end up with five basic responses to conflict – avoidance, accommodation, competition, compromise, and collaboration.

When we do not care about the personal relationship or the outcome, **avoidance** makes sense. Although in truth, most of us avoid when we *do* care, because of our fear of conflict. So we ignore and wait, or move on. We also stonewall, in other words, we remain present in the conversation but shut down and become barely responsive.

Accommodation is appropriate when we care about the relationship but not the outcome. And yet, there are dangers when one person in a relationship is always accommodating and the other is oblivious to or non-caring of this fact.

Accommodators should be careful not to say 'yes' when they really mean no. Nor should they be tolerant in all situations. No one likes being taken for granted, and eventually the proverbial straw lands on the camel's back. At that point, accommodators usually lose their patience and overreact. Then they are in the ballpark for a fight, which brings us to the next basic response to conflict. **Competition**, as an expression of the fight strategy, only makes sense when we care about the outcome but not the relationship. But how often is this the case in the workplace?

Physical workplace violence is still a reality as a destructive way to address conflict. However, it is more likely that the forms of fight behavior encountered are communicative, such as blame, personal attacks and defensiveness.

When we blame, we hold the other person responsible for a situation. Blame typically elicits defensiveness and is usually based on our cognitively biased, assumption-laden interpretation of the facts. It reduces the likelihood of the participants being open to believing each other and to learning about what is really going on.

Further, blame causes the participants to be afraid and unwilling to openly share information pertaining to their contribution to the conflict situation. To solve problems you need good information, without which there can be no real and lasting solution. If you are focused on blame, you are focused on finger-pointing and defensiveness. The appropriate focus should be on fixing the problem.

Personal attacks are critical comments that suggest that something is wrong with a person's character or personality. An example would be calling someone 'stupid'. Mediators need to address these as 'identity' or 'face' issues and should work hard to minimize them, as they create situations that are both negative and embarrassing. Personal attacks also invite defensiveness.

Defensiveness is intimately linked with fear. It starts as a desire to protect ourselves. When we do not believe we are responsible for a situation, or when we perceive a personal attack which threatens our identity or an important relationship, we feel justified in defending ourselves. This leads to the basic spiral dynamic of unproductive conflict. The defensive response is misinterpreted as a counterattack, and the cycle of conflict escalates. If not managed carefully, a mutually destructive power struggle is set in motion.

A key insight from Gottman's research on relationships in conflict is the importance he attaches to restraining a defensive reaction, whether emotionally or behaviorally, even when you perceive yourself to be attacked.[6] If the reactive conflict cycle is not broken, it can escalate towards more aggression and even physical violence.

In most workplace situations, the reality is that both the relationship and the outcome are important. That is why the closely related concepts of **compromise** and **collaboration** are so important. Compromise refers to when a fair and equitable split is sought. It is especially common when a limited resource, such as money, is at stake. Collaboration is about working together, including when we are in conflict. Participants collaborate when they merge resources to reach a common goal that satisfies their respective needs.

There are two collaborative behaviors that are important for the success of the mediation process – negotiation and forgiveness. The former takes place in the external world and attempts to be rational, while the latter is usually internal (although it may also have an external dimension). Forgiveness works with emotions and feelings. Ideally, both these behaviors are embarked upon eventually if not always simultaneously, and usually for a number of good reasons.

Negotiation

"A negotiation is an interactive communication process that may take place whenever we want something from someone else or another person wants something from us."
G. Richard Shell

Disputes are the stuff of negotiation. We negotiate to reach agreement, and when we cannot agree, we defer to a higher authority. We are all aware, to differing degrees, of the numerous moments in our lives when we have negotiated. In essence, negotiation is taking place every time there is an exchange, a debate or a discussion about how to meet our respective needs.

For the most part, we are socialized to be competitive, and led to believe that it is natural. Yet, as we better understand the complexity of social relationships, we see that it is not that simple. Competition and collaboration can and do coexist. How we negotiate is what matters. This 'how' is often framed as a simple choice between competition and collaboration. The reality is more subtle, with participants at times orienting in different directions and exhibiting a wide range of conflict-handling behaviors.

You are the mediator and therefore need to be an inspiring beacon of hope. You should orient and continually reframe towards collaborative or principled negotiation. Try to embrace the theory articulated by Fisher, Ury and Patton in *Getting to YES*; namely, that the key to problem solving in a conflict situation is to focus on the participants' underlying needs.[7] Once these have been identified, you can generate a range of potential solutions from which they can choose. In the event of them becoming stuck, a principled approach is advocated rather than an escalation to power. The authors suggest applying mutually acceptable standards to guide the conversation about fairness, and to talk about what each participant will do in the absence of an agreement. Both their best and worst alternatives to an agreement should be put forward. These alternatives are now known in the mediation profession as BATNA and WATNA, where BATNA means 'Best Alternative to a Negotiated Agreement' and WATNA means 'Worst Alternative to a Negotiated Agreement'.

Mediators who embrace this approach to collaborative negotiation describe themselves as facilitative problem-solving mediators. They help participants to first identify their needs regarding all the discreet issues that need to be addressed. Once this has been done, they help them to brainstorm solutions. This is at the heart of the problem-solving process. I will use the following image, called the Problem-Solving Two Step, to explain the process. Despite its simplicity (or perhaps because of it), it is a very powerful process and central to the model of mediation that I articulate in this book. It is the basic logic of the book, *Getting to YES*.

The Problem-Solving Two Step

Participant A's needs | Participant B's needs

Brainstorm options (potential solutions)

*
*
*

The Problem-Solving Two Step consists of a T-bar and a horizontal line. The T-bar helps us to organize the participants' needs. On the left we record the needs of Participant A, and on the right those of Participant B. We then brainstorm solutions that will best satisfy both sets of needs. The joint nature of the brainstorming endeavor is reflected in the fact that the vertical dividing line of the T-bar is gone.

I sometimes tell the following wonderfully simple story (you have probably heard or read a version of it before): You come home after a long day at work. All you want is peace and quiet. When you open your front door, however, you immediately hear a din from the kitchen. Your children are arguing about who is to have the last orange in the house. Assuming you cannot get more oranges, what do you do?

Most participants suggest that an acceptable solution would be to compromise and to halve the orange. At this point, I remind them of the simple rule about dividing things – that conflict is prevented if one person cuts and the other one chooses.

There is more to the story. I tell them that after the cutting and choosing process, your daughter takes her half, squeezes out the juice, and drinks it. Your son, however, starts to grate the zest for a cake he is baking. This ending shows how we all have differing needs.

This story is useful in that it emphasizes two key lessons about conflict. The first is that, as discussed earlier in this chapter, we need to be careful about making assumptions, especially about what others need. The second is that, as an approach to negotiating conflict, we need to focus on each other's respective needs rather than make demands and threats.

Demands are predetermined outcomes. They are specific and definite, require justification, and are often seen as threatening. They therefore tend to lead to defensiveness. Needs are the underlying reasons for demands being made. There are four types of needs – substantive, relational, identity and process.[8] (The authors use the term 'interests' interchangeably with 'goals'. I use the term 'needs' interchangeably with both 'interests' and 'goals'.) **Substantive** needs relate to the issue or topic at hand that requires resolution. **Relational** needs focus on how we treat one another. **Identity** needs address the participants' reputations and how they prefer to be seen. **Process** needs involve how we interact and go about doing things.

My favorite example of the Problem-Solving Two Step is from a mediation I once conducted between the members of a tenants' association and the owners of an apartment building. Many of the tenants had been in their rent-controlled apartments for over twenty years.

We held our first meeting in an office at the city hall and made good progress. At the next meeting, the members of the tenants' association arrived half an hour late. After they had sat down and I had welcomed everyone, their spokesperson stood up. He pounded the table and, in a loud and angry voice, demanded that all future meetings take place at the apartment block.

"Getting here is really difficult," he said. "As you can see, most of us are elderly and struggle getting around. We refuse to meet here again."

His demand was clear. On the surface, he was displaying anger. And he and the other tenants had a need – an accessible venue for the meetings. Before the owners could respond, I acknowledged that our meeting venue was not suitable for the tenants and that a venue that provided easier *access* was needed. (Now was not the time to probe beneath his anger. The first step involves acknowledging, allowing, and reframing to the valid underlying needs.)

"Yes," he said, sitting down.

Next, I turned to the owners of the apartment block and asked them what their needs were as regards the meeting location. I asked whether they had any concerns about changing the meeting venue to the apartment block.

They said that they enjoyed the drive to the venue and had no issues with access. They liked this location but felt that it did not have to be here. Talking and working something out was more important.

Great, I thought, this is helpful. Then, the younger of the two owners leaned forward and cleared his throat.

"While it is true that we are the owners and should therefore have no objection to meeting at the apartment block, when we met there in the past, the tenants had the home advantage," he said.

"It sounds like a venue that is *neutral* is important to you?" I asked, expectantly.

"Yes," he replied.

"Thanks for sharing what it is you both need in respect of a meeting venue. So, the location needs to be *accessible* to the residents and *neutral* for the owners in order to be suitable for our mediation?" I clarified.

This information about the venue was needed in order to complete Step One: the T-bar with both participants' needs clearly identified. Then I moved to Step Two, and asked the participants to brainstorm potential solutions that would meet their mutual needs. I pointed out that the dividing line that was present during the initial inquiry into their needs was now gone, and that together we could brainstorm solutions that would meet everyone's needs. The visual dimension of this is powerful – there is no longer a line that divides them.

It did not take much to get them started, and after a couple of ideas were thrown out, an elderly man who had been quiet until then raised his hand and asked: "What about the church next door? It has a meeting hall that would be suitable for our meetings. Why don't we meet there?"

Signed, sealed and delivered.

If it seems easy, good – because it really is! And at its heart is a simple reorientation away from demands to the underlying needs that are motivating those demands in the first place.

Up until now, I have described negotiation as a collaborative strategy. Yet it can also be approached competitively, as suggested earlier. Most negotiations are a blend of the two. Many mediators are biased in favor of a collaborative approach. However, we need to be conversant with a competitive strategy in order to meet the participants at the place where they are.

As we guide and interact with the interplay between the participants, we need to observe both the collaborative and competitive moments, sometimes in sync, sometimes clashing. We do not rescue either, but we do constantly seek to reframe to collaboration. This applies to both relational and transactional disputes. As has been mentioned before, it is in this regard that we are not balanced. Leaning towards collaboration is part of our stance.

That said, we also need to be mindful of Robert M. Axelrod's tit for tat theory.[9] This is based on an iterative version of the prisoners' dilemma, which is a classic game-theory challenge that explores the tension between competition and collaboration.[10] Axelrod's theory posits that, where collaboration makes sense, start cooperatively and then simply follow what the other person did the last time. In other words, when your collaborative effort is met with a competitive response, you respond competitively in kind, as a way of showing that two can play at this game. If possible, communicate about the mutual limits of competition and encourage collaboration. Always be forgiving and keep the door open to collaboration. However, until mutual collaboration is established, remain vigilant and respond in kind.

As mediators, we can encourage the participants to be collaborative, we can seek to reframe in that direction at every turn, but we cannot make them do anything. At the end of the day, they are responsible for their situation. Sometimes, things appear harsh. Participants play hardball and are willing to use their power to impose solutions that are more favorable to them than if they were to be more conciliatory. Or the consequences of a decision may be harsh, as in the termination of someone's employment. Watching the competitive aspects of nature, like watching a lion kill a zebra, can be difficult. The same is true of mediation.

Forgiveness

"At its essence, forgiveness is a decision to let go of the past… and to tell a new story about what occurred."
Eileen Barker

There are moments that truly inspire and move us as mediators, not just because we have arrived at a creative solution, but also because of the way the participants have embraced the conflict as an opportunity for insight, learning and change. Through the gift of their conflict, they have found peace and acceptance through the transformative process of forgiveness.

The deepest level of forgiveness is the acceptance of life as it is. Then comes forgiving ourselves for expecting life to be different, and finally we get to where most of us start, forgiving the other person for what they did.

When we accept what has happened, including the range of associated emotions we have experienced, we express gratitude for life and stop wishing the situation were different from the way it is.

This arises from a deep and profound insight into reality. It is what Byron Katie encourages us to do in her book, *Loving What Is*.[11] Any pain/discomfort we experience offers us the opportunity to heal our emotional pain – the baggage and the shadows that we still own.

Conflict is an invitation to go within, to unlock the pain of the past, and to heal. And, as Kenneth Cloke wisely reminds us, the conflict has within it the kernels for what we need to learn.[12] When we forgive ourselves, we show compassion for and understanding of ourselves, and trust that we did our best. We stop being insensitive and hard on ourselves, and take into account our challenging life circumstances. We are no longer our own worst critic. When we forgive the other person who apparently caused us harm, we make peace in the world. It is always worth pondering the miracle that when two people forgive each other on their own, they can completely resolve a conflict.

Forgiveness does not mean we forget, or that we condone. We do not even need an apology in order to forgive, although a sincere apology is a powerful force in its own right. When we forgive each other, we realize that the other person has also suffered and has found a way to forgive. In that sense, nothing is unforgiveable. Rather, forgiveness is a gift we give to others and to ourselves. We take back our power, reconnect with our original positive intention, and repackage our past.

Fred Luskin, a pioneer in the field of forgiveness, sees it as a decision we take to reduce the negative impact of our grievance.[13] He suggests that forgiveness is the reversal of the grievance process. When we experience pain or suffering, we take it personally and blame others for how we are feeling. We tell ourselves a story in which we are the victim. We are aggrieved.

When we forgive, we undo this grievance process. Instead of taking things personally, we recognize that things happen, but that these things (the ten percent) are seldom as problematic as our own reaction (the ninety percent). So, when we forgive, we take responsibility for our own feelings. We retell our story, no longer as a victim, but with a deeper understanding of the significance of the event to our lives.

Ultimately, forgiveness represents a conflict resolution path that we can take on our own, to make peace with what has happened and to chart a happier future.

[1] Beisser, A., 'The paradoxical theory of change', in Fagan & Shepherd (eds), 1970.
[2] Chopra, 2010: 42.
[3] Covey, 2011.
[4] Thomas & Kilmann, 1974.
[5] Hiam, 1999.
[6] Gottman, 1999: 37.
[7] Fisher, Ury & Patton, 1991.
[8] Wilmot & Hocker, 2011: 71.
[9] Axelrod, 1984.
[10] See: http://en.wikipedia.org/wiki/Prisoner%27s_dilemma.
[11] Katie, 2002.
[12] Cloke, 2001.
[13] Luskin, 2002.

Chapter 4

Key Communication Skills

*"The single biggest problem in
communication is the illusion
that it has taken place."*
George Bernard Shaw

Mediators are the custodians of the communication flow. They need to pay close attention to communication, both their own communication skills and the communication dynamics of the participants. They should strive to model clear communication that supports collaborative action, and be very aware of the challenge Shaw describes in the quote above. They should also be aware that to manage the conversation in a manner that maintains focus and supports resolution is a skill that matures over time.

Most mediators consider empathic listening to be their core skill. In addition, the advanced listening skill of reframing is vital. Mediators need to constantly reframe what they hear in order to discharge unnecessary negativity and personal attacks and thereby enable the conflict to be worked on productively. This is one of the most active ways in which they engage in the conflict. Mediators also need to ask a lot of questions, not to satisfy their curiosity but to support the conflict-resolution process. And when they need to assert themselves or be persuasive, mediators are tactful communicators.

This chapter focuses on the key communication skills that support the mediation process. Each of these skills is reviewed from the perspective of the mediator.

Empathic listening

"The most basic of all human needs is the need to understand and be understood. The best way to understand people is to listen to them."
Ralph Nichols

Empathic (or reflective) listening is central to the work of the mediator. As an intervention tool, it is second to none for its ability to build trust and confidence. It enables mediators to demonstrate that they grasp what is going on and understand the participants' perspective – their needs, thoughts and feelings.

This kind of listening builds on closed-loop communication, which requires that the listener be able to demonstrate understanding of what has been said by reflecting the essence of the message back to the speaker. As empathic listeners, mediators do not simply attend to the factual content of what is being said. They also pay special attention to the underlying and often unstated emotional content. It is this latter emphasis that gives empathic listening its name.

When we empathize with someone, our goal is to reflect the other person's emotions and their intensity accurately. We should empty our mind and listen to the speaker with our whole being so that we can show, in a respectful manner, that we have a sense of what that person is experiencing.

Paraphrasing (or summarizing) is the key way in which we demonstrate that we have understood the speaker. This does not require a restatement of every word, but rather an overview or outline of what has been said. Importantly, it accurately condenses what has been stated. It is an opportunity for the speaker to determine whether s/he has been heard and understood. For example, the mediator may say: *"These seem to be the main points you have covered so far (content), and I hear that you are very troubled (feelings) about not knowing what to expect (needs)."*

We use our social awareness skills and monitor each participant's facial expressions and gestures for feeling cues. We may ask ourselves what we would feel in the circumstances, but should be careful not to transpose this onto the speaker. In reflecting back the emotional content, we should avoid statements like 'I understand' or 'I know just how you feel'.

In addition to empathizing, we should validate. This means we acknowledge the validity of the person's experience. For example, we may say: *"In essence, what you are saying is that you are angry, and I can see that makes perfect sense to you, based on what you have just shared."*

Inexperienced mediators are often afraid to validate in case it creates the appearance of agreement and/or bias. However, you can anticipate this danger by reassuring both participants that your goal is to understand, not to agree, and that you will be doing that for both of them. Ultimately, the proof of the pudding is in the eating, because the second participant's turn will come. Be sure to validate equally for both participants. When we remember the Gestalt theory of change (that people can change when they are allowed to experience their feelings – see page 28), we appreciate why this is such a powerful technique.

To be able to accurately reflect back in an empathetic manner, we must give our full physical, mental and emotional attention to the speaker. Our body language should communicate the careful attention we are paying to the person who is talking. We need to be fully absorbed, and yet we should also (in a peripheral manner) pay attention to and sense how the other participant is faring.

Mediators should encourage the participants through the unobtrusive use of words, sounds and gestures. We can use words and phrases like 'yes', 'I see', 'mm-hmm', 'go on', 'tell me more', etc. We can also use positive body cues at appropriate points, such as nods and smiles.

To signal your interest, you should lean slightly towards the speaker while maintaining an open, relaxed posture. You need to keep your physical movement to a minimum and avoid distracting or ambiguous gestures. Remember to look for opportunities to subtly mirror the communication behavior and language use of the speaker. Try to match rather than mix your metaphors, whether they be visual, auditory or kinesthetic. Be careful not to interrupt the flow of the conversation, and allow pauses.

If you take notes, do so unobtrusively after having first explained their purpose and assuring confidentiality. Note taking is a powerful tool for focus and supports accurate summaries. In addition to recording exactly what people say, note-taking helps to organize your identification and understanding of feelings, assumptions and needs.

Reframing

"We can complain because rose bushes have thorns, or rejoice because thorn bushes have roses."

Abraham Lincoln

Reframing is a tool we use to change the view of something. It recognizes that the frame we place to make sense of an event, situation or relationship is not neutral. The decision as to which frame to place therefore involves a conscious choice.

The idiom 'to kill two birds with one stone' can be reframed as 'to open two doors with one key'. The meaning may be the same, but the flavor of the two frames is very different. In the same way, while the phrase 'he never listens' could mean the same thing as 'you need to be heard', the former is framed as an attack, while the latter as a validation.

Which frame best supports resolution is a key question for mediators. Your task is to support the participants to experience a shift, whether it pertains to how they perceive the conflict situation, how they feel about one another, or how they view the world.

A reframe from a negative to a positive perception removes the sting. In the context of conflict resolution, the **primary** reframe is from conflict as a problem to conflict as an opportunity. This is not easy to appreciate when it is your conflict. That is why you need to be very careful not to appear patronizing.

Often, reframing can also be conceptualized as refocusing because the effect of the reframe is a new focus. Two 'refocuses' that are especially important for mediators involve the reframe from past to future, and that from demands to needs. Mediators point out that the past is gone and at best can serve to teach us lessons. By contrast, the future represents where the participants are going, and has the potential of being something better. As mediator, encourage the participants to choose a future orientation.

The reframe or refocus from demands to needs is paramount for mediators who use a problem-solving methodology. Many of those who do will recognize this idea from *Getting to YES*.[1] In the book, the authors talk about 'positions' and 'interests'. In my experience, people better understand the synonymous terms 'demands' and 'needs'.

Mediators acknowledge the respective demands made by each participant, and invite both to also look at the needs that are motivating them to make these demands. Demands are predetermined and prescriptive. They are also closed and threatening. By contrast, when we talk about needs, we discover that we all have them. This refocus is liberating.

We can also reframe the definition of the conflict from a combative to a collaborative one that is most amenable to creative resolution. We reframe as a simple way of holding the mutuality of the challenge in view, so that participants see what they can do together to resolve the conflict. For example, instead of defining the conflict as 'you have to…' we define it as 'how best can we…'.

In addition, how the individual issues are framed will significantly impact the ability of the participants to approach a conflict. The issues, as a description of what the participants need to resolve, should evoke a cooperative (not combative) reaction.

Much reframing, by changing the view into a more positive one, defuses negative and toxic communication behaviors, such as insults and verbal attacks. Reframing a statement helps to acknowledge feelings, validate needs and orient solutions to the future. Be sure to be as balanced and neutral as possible.

Here is an example of reframing. During a mediation, a supervisor says to you about her employee: "I refuse to work with him. He is certifiably incompetent. He never follows instructions and I do not know how many times I have had to bail him out of trouble!"

You sense her desperation and anxiety at the prospect of having to continue working with this employee. Your reframe may go something like this: *"You sound desperate. Having employees who know what they are doing is important. Not being able to expect that they will listen and follow instructions is worrying. You hope for relationships with your employees that are built on trust, and want to feel comfortable that they are able to do the job."*

One way to think of reframing is like the martial art of aikido. Instead of meeting negativity with equal force, which sets up unhelpful, eddy-like resistance patterns, you meet the negative energy, acknowledge it, and step aside to help it on its way.

Reframing provides insight into the role of the mediator as an intervener who engages with the conflict and seeks to move things in a productive direction. As you reframe, you need to be sensitive to the suitability and acceptability of the reframes. You may suggest a reframe, but the participants should decide as to its efficacy.

Most fundamentally, mediators use reframing to shift a negative perception to a positive one. A reframe is always a movement from one thing to another thing, for instance:

- competition to collaboration
- protection to learning
- blame to trust
- confusion to clarity
- doubt to certainty
- destructive to creative
- helpless to confident
- arrogant to vulnerable
- unique to normal
- external to internal.

Asking questions

"Problems that remain persistently insoluble should always be suspected as questions asked in the wrong way."
Alan Watts

Mediators need to ask a lot of questions. But they should not interrogate, humiliate and embarrass the participants. There should be a reason for every question, one that supports the mediation process. Mediators should not ask questions to satisfy their random curiosity. Asking questions is not an opportunity to make a statement or express an opinion. Nor is it a way to communicate how you feel. Rather, questions are a way to discover information that will help you to understand accurately the needs, beliefs or feelings of the participants.

Questions are powerful tools to establish focus and are strongly suggestive of what you consider relevant. However, they can put a participant off track. Try not to intimidate the participant with persistent questions. Sometimes, it pays to be patient and to wait and see if your questions are eventually answered.

Mediators can ask questions in a variety of ways. **Open-ended** questions are a great way to get participants talking openly, especially at the outset of the mediation when they are sharing their perspectives of what has happened: *"How do you see things?"* **Closed-ended** questions expect a 'yes' or 'no' answer, or a short phrase. They are helpful when you seek confirmation: *"Is this helping?"* After the question has been answered, you have an opportunity to influence what happens next. **Probing** questions help you to understand the deeper issues, but they involve risk. *"Why?"* is a powerful probing question that mediators use to uncover underlying needs. *"What will you do if you do not agree?"* is a question that forces participants to consider the consequences of not agreeing. **Leading** questions are useful when you want to confirm something, or test a hypothesis: *"Am I correct in assuming that keeping your job is important to you?"*

As you move through the stages of a typical mediation, you will ask a variety of questions tailored to the needs of the moment.

Assertion: 'I' statements, and saying 'no'

"A 'no' uttered from deepest conviction is better and greater than a 'yes' merely uttered to please, or what is worse, to avoid trouble."
Mahatma Gandhi

Mediators need to be able to role model and coach effective communication behavior. This includes being able to assert yourself and maintain your boundaries. At times, you may need to let either or both of the participants know how their behavior has impacted you, and to request a change.

The current high point in the development of our communication technology for giving feedback is what is called the 'I' statement. Mediators ought to use them, and also encourage participants to use them. 'I' statements are different from 'you' statements in that the latter shut down communication. They are therefore ineffective communicators of what people really need, or want changed. They are also blaming and make people defensive.

By contrast, 'I' statements open up communication. They require you to be honest and direct, and include an unspoken request for what you need. Marshall Rosenberg's book, *Nonviolent Communication*, is based on this simple 'I' statement technology. It requires that we are able to do four things: to describe what it is we are observing; to identify how we feel about what we have observed; to articulate our needs that are not being met and which give rise to our feelings; and to describe the concrete actions we need to move forward.[2] The four elements that play out in this formula are:

- When... (describe behavior in non-blaming terms)
- I feel... (describe your feelings)
- Because... (describe the impact on your needs)
- Make a positive behavior request.

For example: "I feel frustrated when you start talking before I have finished because I forget what I wanted to say. I would appreciate it if you could let me finish talking first."

When coaching participants in the use of 'I' statements, be sure to alert them to the common mistake of saying 'I feel like...' or 'I feel that...'.[3] The words that follow these formulations are seldom descriptive of what people are feeling, for example, the following sentence does not describe feelings: "I feel that you should have supported me in the meeting."

Saying 'no' is a key assertion skill that is linked to knowledge of your boundaries. For example, what would you do if a participant asked you to make a decision? Or if you were asked by a friend to divulge what had happened in a private mediation? Would you say 'no'? Saying 'no' is appropriate when people make requests that would violate our reasonable and lawful boundaries.

In his new book, *The Power of a Positive No*, William Ury reminds us that when we say 'no' to something, we are saying 'yes' to something else.[4] Communicating this with care and kindness can make all the difference. For example: *"I have committed to keeping the communications in the mediation confidential. Keeping my word is important. I hope you will understand why I cannot talk about what happened."*

Managing flow

"The quality of the imagination is to flow and not to freeze."
Ralph Waldo Emerson

Mediators exercise much of their influence through the way they manage the flow of communication. Some mediators are more structured and controlling, while others believe you should follow, not lead.

This is where your intuitive sensitivity and imagination come into play. You are aware of a variety of qualities that could describe the communication dynamics in a mediation. Like a river, sometimes things appear to flow smoothly and you hardly need to say a word. At other times, things are languid and everything feels heavy and difficult, or the nervousness/excitement is palpable, like water splashing over rocks. Be comfortable with it all, and be ready to intervene and shift the dynamics if and when you need to. This means that you need to be able to both let go and take control. Remember, your role is to support the participants to resolve their conflict.

What is important is to let the participants finish speaking and give them the time to find their way. Too often, in the haste to cut to the chase, we miss vital communications. As Gregorio Billikopf would say: "Allow the pause!".[5] The pause is often a time of mental regrouping in which we make sense of what we have just heard ourselves say. Pausing and reflecting often sets participants up to take the deeper path to what is really going on. Simply put, be comfortable with silence – it creates space for awareness.

If the conversation appears to lose focus, you may want to check in with the participants to see if what they are talking about is relevant and necessary.

If one of the participants is being repetitive, consider first the need to demonstrate that you have understood. If the repetition continues after you have listened actively, try something along these lines: *"It is clear that this is very important to you. Is there anything else that is also important for us to understand?"*

Notice how the closed-ended question will restore control to you as the mediator.

In the case of repetitiveness, you may want to try another tactic altogether – a global summary that attempts to create a working frame to look at the issues of both participants in a balanced way. For example, you may say: *"You both seem to be saying that a solution needs to be found regarding the maintenance of the calendar. You have different solutions in mind. We are here to find the most creative solution using all your available resources."*

Sometimes, the challenge is to draw someone out and make sure that there is more balance to the flow. Keys to this challenge are patience and being comfortable with silence.

---

1   Fisher, Ury & Patton, 1991: 40.
2   Rosenberg, 1999: 6-7.
3   *Ibid.*: 41.
4   Ury, 2007: 16-20.
5   Billikopf, 2009: 35-37.

Chapter 5
The Mediation Process

*"Mediation is a conciliatory process in which an acceptable
third party intervenes in the conflict or disputes of participants
with the goal of supporting them to reach agreement."*
John Ford

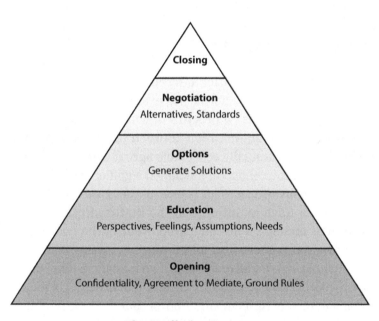

The Mediation Process

In this chapter, I review my definition of mediation and explain the
five basic phases of the mediation process, as shown in the illustration
above. I also discuss the caucus and how it can be used before the
mediation as part of convening, during the mediation as part of the
education phase, and after the joint mediation sessions as part of the
follow-up process. The chapter ends with a consideration of the
involvement of management champions.

A conciliatory process

Most simply, the word conciliate means 'to bring together in order to placate'. In the *Dictionary of Conflict Resolution*, Yarn describes conciliation as an act of bringing people together, by a third party who may or may not be neutral, in order to encourage them to settle their dispute.[1]

Mediation is conciliatory, not adversarial. As mediators, we do not impose solutions in the manner associated with an adjudicatory process. Rather, we encourage conciliation through our resonant relationships with the participants.

An acceptable third party

Many definitions of mediation currently in use require that the mediator be neutral. In California, for example, mediation is defined in the evidence code as "a process in which a *neutral* person or persons facilitate communication between the disputants to assist them in reaching a mutually acceptable agreement".[2]

Neutrality in the context of mediation signifies impartiality and a lack of bias and favoritism.[3] This is possible because the neutral third party does not have an interest in the matter. In the workplace, however, HR managers are paid employees of the company. They support the management of all human resources. Although HR managers are there for all employees, line managers often think they are their representatives, and try to get them involved in the day-to-day management of the company. And, of course, these lines blur and differ from company to company. What is clear is that HR managers are not neutral in the strict sense of the word.

However, as Yarn's definition of conciliation reveals, mediators do not have to be neutral. Yet we *do* need to be acceptable to the participants, and the participants need to decide this. What is important is that we strive to be neutral (although I prefer the term 'balanced'). We should be willing to disclose potential conflicts of interest, and if we are no longer acceptable to the participants after this disclosure, we should withdraw. Remember, we are there in the service of the participants.

If an HR mediator has been coaching a manager regarding the handling of a performance issue, other employees may perceive that HR mediator to be biased. However, another HR manager who has been uninvolved in the issue may well be perceived as acceptable. In some large organizations, HR managers mediate for one another's business groups.

Mediators intervene

In mediation, a third party (the mediator) intervenes. We are not passive; rather, we get involved in the process based on the potential to help. Our interventions include:

- modifying the physical setting
- facilitating communication behavior
- guiding, engaging and supporting the negotiation process
- intervening to address the emotional and mental elements of the conflict.

And immediately after we intervene, we get feedback from the participants. This feedback may simply be silence, or it may be a look. Sometimes, it comes in the form of irritation directed at us. The feedback will indicate whether the intervention is helping or not. If an intervention is not working, we need to do something different. If it is having the desired effect and is soothing and collaborative, we can relax and continue to be present to what is unfolding in the moment.

Mediators discover that, probabilities notwithstanding, interventions have no guaranteed results. We get what we get, and we must meet that reality as it presents itself and move from there. We cannot expect that the intervention we used last week, which worked a certain way with two other participants, will work the same way with the present participants.

We need to be careful not to triangulate. This means we must not take sides, whether through an imbalance of attention or by accepting one participant's view of the problem. We need to intervene in a manner that is perceived to be balanced. This is one of the core aspects of the mediator's stance – the intention to be balanced, and the perception of balance (see Chapter 2, pages 9-10 and 19).

Our interventions ensure that we avoid conflict resolution obstacles. Challenges are inevitable, and when they arise, our interventions need to be measured according to what is needed. We should be able to use interventions to slow things down, and turn attention from one issue to another. In this way, we are more or less directive, yet we should always fall short of imposing a substantive decision regarding the issues.

Even in our non-doing, silent, observing state, we are intervening. In this sense we are very active. Our role is to support the discussion or negotiation in a manner that supports collaboration. The reality is that the participants are usually at different stages of readiness for the mediation process, and buy into a collaborative approach to differing degrees.

Some have a core that says: "I want to fight." Others want to run. Some are emotionally mature, while others want to collaborate but do not know how. Still others know how but are unwilling to do so. Mediators meet it all. We need to be comfortable facilitating collaborative and competitive negotiations, as well as a mixture of both.

Over time, we begin to trust our ability to maintain the perception of balance in our mediations. Our interventions become sensitive to what is needed, and our behavior makes it apparent that our deepest intention is to be fair to both participants while supporting their resolution process. As long as we have assumed the mediator's stance and are following the steps in the mediation process, things generally work out. I estimate that more than eighty percent of mediations worldwide produce agreements.

Conflict and/or dispute

Conflict theorists distinguish a conflict from a dispute: "A dispute begins when someone makes a claim or demand on another, who rejects it."[4] According to this distinction, then, a dispute is a conflict that has escalated to the point that positions have hardened and there is a disagreement. Someone has made a demand, and someone has refused to meet it.

We will discover that it is much easier to intervene early, before a conflict has risen to the level of a dispute.

Personality conflicts are good examples of conflicts that mediators can nip in the bud. Participants in these conflicts need to talk, clear the air, and recommit to working productively together, taking into account the various insights that have been generated by the mediation to support more ease in the relationship. There may or may not be a dispute involved. If there is, the good news is that the mediation process is especially adept at working with disputes. The dramatic increase in the use of mediation by the courts around the world is testament to this dispute-resolving ability.

Consent of the participants

Mediation requires participation. Generally, voluntary participation works best. It is better to gain the consent of both people to participate in the mediation rather than to require it.

In the workplace, subtle pressure is often placed on employees to agree to mediate, especially when it is seen to represent a lifeline for one or both of them. The same applies to managers. There is a belief that if an employee wants to talk with the support of a mediator, the manager should go along with this, despite the denial of any responsibility for the problem.

The mediator's support

Our role as mediator is to support the participants, not to take responsibility or to decide for them. It is always good to remind ourselves that it is not our conflict or dispute. It exists between the participants. We need to support them through the application of a variety of well-timed interventions, all of which are intended to help. We should always be careful to gain and work with the consent of the participants through our openness to feedback, and, of course, transparent and direct communication.

We should also be clear that it is in regard to process that we are the least balanced. We have our expertise, and we know the value of the mediation process. It is precisely because we offer the hope of resolution, through our skills and our knowledge, that the participants can trust the mediation process.

This trust must be honored and treated with care. As mediators, we bring our process, and yet, paradoxically, it must remain the participants' process. If we are to use our frames and interventions, then we should earn that right, as we slowly develop trust and confidence with each participant.

Reaching agreement

It is universally understood that the goal of mediation is to reach a voluntary agreement. Yet, despite mediation, some participants do not get there. In effect, they agree to resolve their conflict by another means. When this happens, mediators should be careful not to push too hard for agreement. We support participants to reach agreements that make sense to them. This may include presenting them with robust, reality-checking questions. However, at all times, we need to be clear that our role is *not* to decide.

Ultimately, if the participants do not agree, we as mediators need to know that at least we made them look clearly at the conflict, and that their choice is an informed one. It is irrelevant that we may have chosen differently had it been our conflict. It is not for the mediator to agree, but for the participants to reach the agreements they want to reach.

The basic mediation process

This can be described as a linear process that follows five discreet phases to support the participants to reach agreement. It helps if the mediator has confidence in these basic steps.

1. The **Opening Phase** includes convening the mediation, the room set-up and the opening statement. We also consider confidentiality as an important trust-building step in the mediation set-up.
2. At one level, the **Education Phase** constitutes the T-bar, as described in the Problem-Solving Two Step (see pages 36-37). During this phase, which most mediators agree should be approached slowly and with sensitivity, both participants take turns narrating their perspective of the situation, how they think, feel, and what their needs are in order to move forward.

3. The **Option-generation Phase** is essentially Step Two of the Problem-Solving Two Step. Once a variety of potential solutions have been identified through a brainstorming session, or naturally through the exploration of solutions, the participants negotiate agreements.

4. During the **Negotiation Phase**, participants consider the consequences of not agreeing, and gain comfort by using acceptable standards. If needs be, the mediator uses impasse-breaking intervention techniques to support the emergence of agreements.

5. During the final **Closing Phase**, any agreements are drafted and signed. Ideally, there is an associated ritual, such as a handshake.

As you can see from the illustration below, the basic mediation process is represented graphically as a pyramid. This suggests the linear movement of the process towards agreement at the top. The opening phase is the foundation on which everything rests. In an actual mediation, there is a degree of fluidity. For instance, you may be in the negotiation phase when you realize that you need to establish a new ground rule, which properly speaking is part of the opening phase.

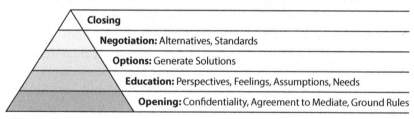

The Mediation Process

The caucus

"In caucusing, the third-party neutral meets separately with each disputant, in the absence of the other contending party. In pre-caucusing, these separate meetings take place before the mediator brings the contenders into a joint session."
Gregorio Billikopf

One of the mediator's most powerful tools is the **caucus**, a private and confidential meeting with each of the participants. When mediators caucus, they are not at liberty to reveal what the participants have said without their express consent. While the caucus may be a powerful intervention, it remains an intervention and is therefore not a necessity in every mediation.

In caucusing, it is essential that you be clear with each participant about what they are happy for you to share with the other. It is therefore good practice to summarize your understanding of what you may share before leaving the room. It is helpful to write things down. Trust is vital, so be careful not to betray confidences by sharing things you have been asked not to share.

A real danger with caucusing is that we inadvertently create the impression that we are on a particular participant's side. Be careful of this. As you validate, remind the participant that you will be conducting the same kind of meeting with the other participant. Monitor the time you spend with each participant. Ideally, you should spend similar periods of time with each, although in reality this is not always possible.

Although the caucus is commonly used during the negotiation phase, it may be used at any time during the mediation process. There are three junctures at which it makes sense to ask whether the caucus should be used. The first is prior to the first joint session. In this case, it is called the convening caucus (or, as Gregorio Billikopf calls it, the pre-caucus).[5] When used here, it is really a continuation of the convening process. The second juncture is immediately after the opening statement. Instead of going into a joint session, the mediator meets with each of the participants in private as part of the education phase. The third juncture is at the end of the entire process, as a check-in to see how things are going, as part of the follow-up meeting process. All three of these situations are dealt with in Chapter 11.

Participation: involving a management champion

It is especially helpful in the context of relational conflicts where behavioral changes are contemplated to include a manager for the duration of the opening statement and until the Agreement to Mediate is signed. Often, the manager to whom both participants report is the person who has encouraged, or even authorized, the mediation.

The manager helps to frame what the mediation needs to address, and empowers the mediator to work with the participants to do so. In effect, the mediator is stepping into the shoes of the manager in respect of the issues at stake.

Beginning the process with the manager present allows the mediator to be crystal clear about who is responsible for what. The mediator needs to explain to the participants that this situation applies only for the duration of the mediation, and only as it pertains to the issues authorized to be addressed.

As mediator, express the hope that at the end of the mediation process the participants will invite the manager back to the signing ceremony, where s/he will discover what agreements the two of them have worked out. Meeting with the manager makes sense where you want to maximize factors supporting a high level of commitment.

After this opening, which includes the signing of the Agreement to Mediate, you move on to the education phase. If the mediation does indeed produce agreements which the participants are ready to sign, you set up a final meeting, to which you invite the manager. The role of the manager at this meeting is to express appreciation that the employees have resolved the conflict, and to commit to supporting them to honor their agreements. It is a time for celebration.

Be careful how you manage the involvement of the manager. There may still be residual tendencies for one-upmanship. Work to ensure that you are ready, that the participants are ready, and that inviting the manager back is low risk for them. The last thing you want is a flare up with the manager present.

---

[1]   Yarn, 1999: 102
[2]   Section 1115 of the California Evidence Code, 1998.
[3]   Yarn, 1999: 322.
[4]   Ury, 1988.
[5]   Billikopf, 2009.

Chapter 6
The Opening Phase

*"The opening statement is your
opportunity to reduce anxieties and
address any concerns about mediation
before the session begins."*

Joe Torres

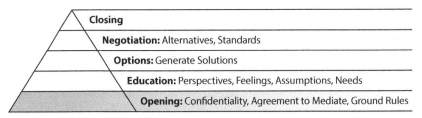

The Mediation Process

The mediator meets the participants in disarray, tension and uncertainty. Usually, negative attributions are mutual, and both participants are often stuck in a form of righteousness. Your goal as mediator is to meet the participants where they are and to support them to move themselves to being composed, engaged and decisive so that they can participate effectively in the mediation process. In essence, you have to get them ready to have a 'difficult' conversation about a conflict and to deal with the inevitable hurt feelings and troubling thoughts that will go along with it.

As was outlined in the previous chapter, the opening phase of the mediation includes convening the process, the room set-up and the opening statement.

1. Convening the process

If employees need to resolve an important issue but have not been able to do so on their own, it makes sense to turn to a mediator.

Mediation works best when both disputants perceive that it is in their best interests to participate in mediation voluntarily.

Convening the process focuses on how you get disputants to become willing participants at the mediation table. The interest in mediation is not always mutual, nor is it always valued in the same way. Often, one of the participants will not want to mediate and will resist. If this occurs, remind yourself of what Ken Cloke says: "Resistance is a sign of an unmet need."[1] Listen empathically to the participant who has concerns, and work to support the satisfaction of that person's needs.

It may be a manager who does not see the need to sit down with the employee, or is in fact insulted and humiliated to be in this situation in the first place. *"You sound pissed off,"* you say, in a way that matches the person's intensity and is culturally appropriate. *"You are busy and are not sure that this is your problem. Do you want to talk about it?"* This approach usually calms and composes the person because you have not met resistance with force, nor have you told anyone what to do.

You have asked a question, to which you will keep returning as you continue to listen empathically to whatever the person is saying. At this stage, you do not need to worry about the conflict. All you need to do is listen, and seek to build trust and confidence. To the extent that you can, keep refocusing the conversation on the option of mediation as a process. At some later point, you will intervene to focus on the question concerning participation in mediation. Trust yourself to know when to do this.

Meet the resistance of all the negatives that are presented. You may have to support the participants in concluding that mediation is not appropriate. You cannot force participation. It may make sense to you, but not necessarily to either or both participants.

Remember, it is not for you to decide. Your role is to support the participants to make an informed decision. And if you eventually get a 'yes', it will be a powerful 'yes'. When this happens, talk about the suitability and benefits of mediation as a collaborative process. Also, point out that mediation makes sense because both an important relationship *and* an important outcome (their work) are at stake.

The information you gleaned as you listened earlier now comes into play as you seek to assuage the possible fears raised.

"The company recognizes that conflict is to be expected and that sometimes employees need support working something out. Our CEO recently encouraged employees to make use of the mediation services that some of the newly trained HR managers, like myself, would be offering. When you agree to mediation, it shows that you are a team player who is willing to listen. That will always count in your favor."

Mostly, when mediation is offered and it makes sense, the opportunity is seized. But not always. It is for this reason that some organizations require management participation where an employee has requested an opportunity to mediate. Short of requiring participation, many organizations will eventually create the expectation that both disputants participate. "It has been decided that mediation would be a good idea for both of you," someone in HR will convey. A little like getting someone to take their medicine so that they can heal!

It is important to realize that when participation in mediation is required, it does not necessarily mean that the outcome of mediation will be an agreement. This aspect of self-determination – the freedom to agree or not – is sacrosanct for the process of mediation. Mediators have an opportunity to adopt the mediation stance when they convene with the participants. We model the values of the mediation process itself as we listen, and then join the possibly hesitant participants as they decide whether to mediate or not.

As mediation becomes more widely used, more people will have had the experience of mediation as a successful process that enabled an informed consumer decision about participation. Hopefully, more people will also be able to distinguish between the mediation process itself and the quality of the mediator. Although many people may have some related knowledge and/or experience of mediation in other settings, workplace mediation is often something that people will be exploring for the first time.

Mediators need to meet the participants where they are, and listen to their reasons not to participate in mediation with sensitivity and care. As we help the participants to sort through their feelings and thoughts about what is best for them, they should start to trust our ability to support them with the actual conflict. The mediator's stance that you adopt ought to put them at ease. If it makes sense to them to mediate, the chances are they will want your support.

Once mediation has been agreed upon, the conversation can turn to more practical matters, such as when and for how long. For relational issues, a series of two-hour meetings works well. But there may be constraints that require you to mediate for shorter or longer sessions. Use good common sense. This is also a time to be alert to any language challenges that may exist, and also to establish any disability needs that would require accommodation.

A best practice is to conduct a convening caucus with each of the participants (discussed in detail in Chapter 11). In essence, this is a continuation of the commitment conversation described above. Once you have the commitment of both participants, consider meeting in private with each of them to hear their perspectives in full, to coach them, and to take the emotional pulse of the conflict. In high conflict situations, you will be glad you did this.

2. Room set-up

Mediations are typically scheduled to start at a particular time in a predetermined location. As the mediator, you will ideally arrive first and set up the room, which should be comfortable and private. You may need to close blinds or windows. If there is a window, position yourself nearest to it so that you are slightly silhouetted and can easily see the participants' expressions.

A table is usually used, but this is not a necessity. Sometimes, to create a more informal atmosphere without the perceived barrier of a table, mediators place chairs in a circle. While a round table is ideal, conference or meeting-room tables are usually rectangular. You can either sit at the end of a rectangular table with the participants opposite one another, or you can sit on the one side with the participants opposite you and next to one another.

Research shows that having the participants sit opposite one another is the most competitive arrangement. You should therefore generally avoid this configuration (Figure 1 on the right).

When you place the participants next to one another, they have the feeling of siding with rather than opposing each other (Figure 2). This is what I do most of the time.

However, many mediators (including myself) will at times position themselves at the end of the table (Figure 1). This may be important when you sense the need to approach the mediation with more formality, and you want to reassure the participants that you are ready to help and guide them.

Gregorio Billikopf suggests that the mediator sits at the far end of the table to emphasize the fact that the mediation process is "party directed".[2] In his opinion, the participants should have to turn their heads to see the mediator (Figure 3).

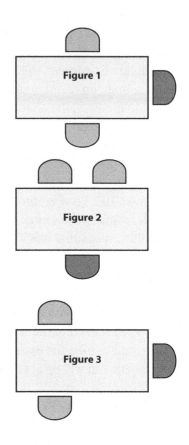

Choose soft chairs over hard, as there is no reason to induce distracting physical discomfort. Armrests are also handy and may minimize the ambiguous crossing of the arms across the chest.

There is no absolute right or wrong where set-up is concerned. Be sensitive to the environment, and set up in a manner that best supports the mediation process. Consider going off site or even outdoors. As long as you are all comfortable and the venue is private enough, use it. Small details in the set up can make a difference, so try to use whatever resources are available to you in the most creative way possible.

3. The opening statement

This is a structured intervention that begins almost every mediation. The form and content of the opening statement may vary. It can be as brief as: *"Welcome, we are here today to identify your issues and to see if you can resolve them. Let us begin!"* Typically, most opening statements are longer!

The opening statement is the point at which the mediator transitions from any small talk and, in effect, starts the session. It is very important to set the right tone from the beginning. Be aware that you will have the attention of the participants to differing degrees. Often, their nervousness will make it difficult for them to focus and pay attention. An effective opening statement accomplishes a number of things:

1. It gives you the opportunity to explain your role, the essence of the mediation process, and how it works so that the participants are ready to engage in the process.
2. It puts the participants at ease and helps them to relax. It also allows them to slowly orient to the reality that they are about to grapple with a topic that has, until now, been difficult. As the mediator, your calm and measured confidence in your abilities and in the mediation process is bound to be infectious.
3. It provides hope. It says yes, we can work things out. There is a way. It is called mediation and here is how it works.
4. It builds rapport and opens the way for the participants to take their first baby steps together. They sign an agreement to mediate, they agree on ground rules, and they are invited to trust the process.
5. It establishes that both participants are committed to mediating their conflict or dispute. They choose to participate.

What to include in your opening statement

I encourage you to draft an opening statement and to rehearse it until you have memorized it. Delivering an effective opening statement confidently will go a long way to comforting the participants. Conversely, consider the impact of a mediator referring to a check list, or reading an opening statement from a script.

Not everything needs to be covered in the opening statement. In fact, it should be less about covering and more about connecting. And if you do want to bring up something later that you may have forgotten to address in the opening statement, you can do so when the need arises.

The following are some of the points you should consider for your opening statement:

1. Introduce yourself

You may need to introduce yourself, especially if someone else has arranged for you to serve as a mediator. Clarify how you would like to be addressed. Say something like: *"Hi, my name is John Ford and I have been asked to be your mediator today. Please feel free to call me John."*

2. Participant introductions

Most of the time, participant introductions are unnecessary. However, it is a good idea to establish how they would like to be addressed. A lot will depend on prior practices. Encourage them to do what feels comfortable.

3. Affirm voluntary participation

Starting early and continuing through the mediation, commend the participants for voluntarily attending the session to find a solution.

"I am encouraged that you have both chosen to mediate. It tells me that you both want to work something out."

Sometimes, to obtain a higher degree of cooperation and to give the participants an opportunity to speak early on in the process, you could ask them to say a word or two about what they hope to achieve by participating in the mediation. In my experience, most people say things like: "I came here today to see if we can resolve things and move forward." Or: "I want to know what happened." Some will also say things like: "I want an apology." Or: "We have to talk about money."

Allowing these short statements gives the participants an early opportunity to contract energetically with one another through the identification of goals. It also gives you the chance to affirm in strong terms how encouraged you are.

"It appears that while you are in conflict, you are both open to working something out. I am encouraged. And in all honesty, I am unaware of any reason for your not being able to work it out."

Be ready to respond to what is happening. Do not be afraid to intervene if the participants start going into too much detail. Gently intervene by summarizing the gist of their goals, secure confirmation that you have indeed understood, thank the participants, and move on.

Always uphold the integrity of the communication process. You want to model clear communication. If, for some reason, your intention in giving them an early opportunity to speak is misunderstood, apologize and use the situation as an opportunity to normalize the challenge of human communication.

4. Frame the conflict

Your goal is to seek the most palatable, inclusive and cooperative frame for the conflict. A future orientation always helps. Suggesting a mutual frame to define the conflict is important too as it directly impacts the participants' ability to approach the conflict productively. A 'neutral' description works best. For example, the conflict can be cast in general terms, such as: *"We are here today to focus on your working relationship and to see what agreements you can reach to help it thrive."*

Sometimes, a more focused frame is appropriate, such as when a specific issue requires attention. You could say: *"We are here today to find a mutually acceptable way to address the most recent performance review."*

5. Explain the mediation process

Without going into too much detail, describe the mediation process and check that the participants understand. They need to know that they are both going to have an opportunity to share their perspectives, and that you as mediator will be actively listening. Once the conflict situation has been fully explored, potential solutions will be sought.

"After I have completed my opening statement, each of you will have an uninterrupted opportunity to share your perspectives of the situation. I encourage you both to identify your needs and talk about how you feel and what you think. After each of you has had a turn, and we have had a full opportunity to explore the situation, we will work together to develop solutions. I may make suggestions, based on what I have seen others do in similar situations, but as I will clarify in more detail later, I will always fall short of telling you what to do."

6. Establish who goes first

Another way to put the participants at ease is by signaling who is going to share their perspective first. This is best addressed after you have explained the mediation process, so that they have had some time to prepare and adjust. The question of who goes first is not set in stone. Two rules of thumb guide the decision: Who took the step to initiate mediation? Who has less power? If you are unsure of who should go first, ask the participants. Allowing them to reach an agreement on this will add to their confidence and build collaborative momentum.

If you have conducted a convening caucus, you may have some information that influences your decision. For example, if one of the participants is contrite about something, perhaps an emotional outburst or an insensitive comment, and wants to apologize, allowing them to go first avoids the other participant having to make an embarrassing accusation.

Here is an example of what you can say if you are going to be directive: *"After I have finished the opening statement and we have signed the Agreement to Mediate, I will ask Sally to share her perspective first. We have to start with someone, and the norm is to start with the person who contacted us in HR to request mediation. This is not set in stone, and if it makes more sense for Harry to go first, we can talk about it."*

Or, if you want them to decide: *"We have to start with one of you. What are your thoughts about who should go first?"*

7. Clarify your role as mediator

Being clear that your role is not to decide is one of the attributes of the mediator's stance. You want the participants to understand that you are not a judge or an arbitrator. And if they cannot work something out, you are not going to impose a decision. Emphasize that they, and not you, are responsible for resolving the conflict. Your role is to support them. It follows that you are not an advocate or representative of either.

"My role is to support you to reach your own agreements. To that extent, you are responsible for any resolution. I am not a judge or an arbitrator. I am also not here in a representative capacity. I expect that both of you are able to speak for yourselves and make your own informed decisions."

8. Mediator balance (omnipartial)

This is your opportunity to empower the participants to decide whether you are conducting the mediation in a balanced fashion. The mediator's intention is to be balanced, neutral, impartial, fair and free of bias. Accomplishing all of this as a matter of fact is unlikely, which is why your intention and the participants' perception are what really matter.

Although I prefer the term 'balance', I encourage you to consider using the other terms, especially if you have a sense that they will resonate well with the participants. If you like the term 'impartial', you can consider describing yourself as 'omnipartial' or 'all-partial'. Sometimes, I say that my goal is to make sure that the process is 'fair to all'.

As you deliver your opening statement, the participants will notice how you balance your gaze so that you are constantly turning from one to the other, not dissimilar to watching tennis. In everything you do, try to embody balance. As you invite the participants to monitor your behavior, request that they give you feedback so that you can adjust, if necessary. What is bothering them or causing them to doubt your balance may be easily addressed.

If it is not, however, and one or both of the participants no longer trusts you, then it is appropriate for you to withdraw and to seek a mediator who is acceptable to them. As difficult as this may be, this is not something to take personally or to get defensive about.

Here is how you may word it: *"As we work together, I am going to do my very best to be balanced and neutral. I want to ensure that this process is fair. My taking sides will not help me and I really have no reason to do so. However, if for any reason you feel that I am taking sides, please let me know. There may be something that I can do to address your concerns. However, if there is nothing I can do, we will need to find a replacement mediator. It is more important that you mediate than that you mediate with me."*

9. Define parameters of confidentiality

Confidentiality and the protection of communications made during mediation are considered key and integral components of the mediation process. Knowing that the process is private and off the record allows the participants to open up and have a free and frank exchange about what is really going on. If employees fear that your notes will find their way into a personnel file, or that what they say will be used against them later on, they will not be open and candid. The goal is to create an environment in which information can be shared without fear of negative consequences.

"To encourage candid and open communication, this mediation process is confidential. What you share here will not be repeated or used against you. I will not be writing a report or discussing the mediation with anyone.

"Your manager/director knows you are here, and will want to see any agreements you work out. I hope you see that this is on a need-to-know basis.

"We will soon sign the Agreement to Mediate. It provides certain exceptions. For example, I am required to report any information that reveals criminal activity or elder or child abuse.

"At a practical level, I wonder if either of you will in the normal course of events want to debrief in confidence with someone close, such as your spouse/partner or mentor. I believe it better to acknowledge this as a reality, and to limit such disclosures to these persons. Do either of you have anyone in mind?"

10. The caucus

This is a powerful intervention, and it is wise to establish it as an option to use. However, failure to mention the caucus during the opening statement does preclude its use later on. To use the caucus, you need to do two things: explain what it is and why it is beneficial, and establish the rules for its use.

"At times, it may make sense for me to meet in private with each of you. We call this a caucus session. I may suggest one, and either of you are welcome to do the same.

"If we do caucus, I will not repeat what you share with me. I will make certain at the end of the private meeting exactly what I may convey to the other, if anything. I will honor your confidences. If I meet with one of you, I will meet with the other too. The same rules will apply. I will hold in confidence whatever is shared."

11. Establish ground rules

Ground rules can be imposed or elicited. As mediator, it is a good idea to identify the ground rules that you want to work with so that if you choose to impose them, you are ready. When we impose ground rules, we have greater control; however, this results in a lower level of co-operation and commitment than when we elicit them.

A sound approach is to combine the two. Invite the participants to generate ground rules that will ensure their safety and comfort, and supplement them with your own, as needed.

"Before we get started, let us consider ground rules. We know the session will be confidential. What other agreements would you like to reach that indicate how we are going to communicate with one another? What is important is that you both feel safe and comfortable. I want to be sensitive to your communication norms. For example, in some cultures, interrupting is a way of showing we are engaged. People from other cultures consider this rude, and prefer to speak in turns. I share this as an example. How will we deal with interruptions? And what other agreements are important to each of you?"

Sometimes, the participants are comfortable proceeding without making explicit ground rules. Be sensitive to ongoing relationships

and the reality that the participants have evolved ways of communicating with one another. It is not your job to impose a particular style
of communication. However, you are responsible for the well-being of
all. When trust levels are low and/or the participants are displaying
strong emotions, be explicit.

If it becomes apparent that the communication dynamics are
problematic and you have started without making ground rules
explicit, trust your intuition and initiate a conversation to establish
ground rules. These empower you as the mediator to hold the participants to their agreements. Be careful not to be too draconian. You do
not want to stifle the communication or over-sanitize it. The challenge
is to allow the 'conflict in the room' without it becoming a free-for-all.
Sample ground rules for you to consider are included as Appendix 2
on page 162.

12. Logistics

Making sure that everyone is clear about the duration of the mediation and when breaks will be taken helps to put the participants at
ease. Uncertainty about logistics adds unnecessary stress. If the
participants are unfamiliar with the meeting venue, orient them to
the bathroom and other amenities.

In some situations it is wise to establish the next meeting date
and time at the start of the session because if things are tense when
you adjourn, at least the next date has been established. However, the
norm is to set a new date at the end of the session.

*"As you know, we have set aside two hours for this session. I am
hopeful that we will be able to work something out in that time.
However, if we are not able to do so, we can arrange another date
and time at the end of this session."*

13. Questions

Give the participants the opportunity to ask clarifying questions and
make comments as you move through your opening statement. When
they share something or ask a question, it allows you to gain valuable
information about how they are feeling and/or how they see things.

Their questions reveal what is on their minds. Be careful to address their questions without being dismissive or patronizing.

"I have been doing a lot of talking. All of this information can be overwhelming. What questions do you have at this time?"

14. Understanding and commitment

After your opening statement and before going any further, establish that the participants understand the process, want to mediate, and want you to be their mediator.

"Now that I have answered your questions, it appears that you both understand what mediation is and want to mediate with me. Is that correct? Are we ready to begin?"

At this point, you hope for affirmations. However, if you sense any hesitation or uncertainty, explore it, and seek to address any resistance before moving forward.

15. Review and sign the Agreement to Mediate (ATM)

It is not always necessary to sign an Agreement to Mediate. Much will depend on the circumstances. For example, if you have an internal mediation program, you may have a standardized ATM that you can use. Where mediation is provided on an *ad hoc* basis, carefully consider whether or not you need an ATM. If you decide to sign an ATM, ensure that you do so before proceeding to matters of substance. A sample ATM that is suitable for use within organizations is included as Appendix 1 on page 159.

If you are using an ATM, make sure that both participants have had an opportunity to review it prior to the mediation. A good practice is to send it out in advance of the mediation meeting. If this has not happened, read through the ATM or highlight the key points. Although it may appear redundant, the points in the ATM should reinforce what you have said and provide additional comfort for the participants.

As mediator, sign the ATM in order to make it crystal clear that you are also bound by the confidentiality provisions.

"Let us take a moment to review and sign the Agreement to Mediate. It establishes the confidentiality of the proceedings and

also confirms what I have been telling you about the mediation process."

After signing, say: *"Now we are ready. Sally, are you ready to share your perspective?"*

---

[1]   Cloke, 2001.
[2]   Billikopf, 2009.

Chapter 7
The Education Phase

"The more time the parties invest in educating each other, the greater chance they will have of developing options and reaching agreements."

Susan Carpenter and William Kennedy

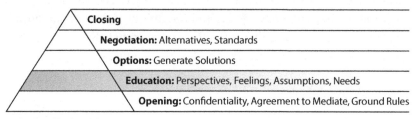

Closing

Negotiation: Alternatives, Standards

Options: Generate Solutions

Education: Perspectives, Feelings, Assumptions, Needs

Opening: Confidentiality, Agreement to Mediate, Ground Rules

The Mediation Process

During this phase, the participants take turns sharing their perspective of the issues at stake. As the quote above suggests, ensuring thoroughness is a good idea, despite any inclinations to 'cut to the chase'. At the end of this phase, both of the participants should be satisfied that they have been heard, and know that their particular issues have been identified. They should also have shared and discovered one another's perspectives of what happened, and what they feel, think and need.

This phase is also an opportunity to support the exploration of how the participants remember and interpret 'the facts', as well as their respective motives or intentions. They will discover things, as each of them reveals what the other did not previously know. They will also review their assumptions about scarcity, interference and compatibility. Your ability as mediator to explore their separate and yet connected realities will influence whether or not they are able to shift their perceptions from 'right and wrong' to 'how best can we'.

Through this sharing of perspectives, emotions will surface about both the issues needing resolution and the experience of the mediation itself. Participating in mediation takes courage. It can be challenging for the participants to remain composed when they relive strong feelings. As mediator, you are responsible for the emotional climate, which you need to manage with care. Continuing to maintain the integrity of the safe mediation space is vital. This is where your emotional agility comes to the fore. When you intervene, do so with sensitivity to the emotional needs of the participants.

Finally, this phase generates the information necessary to use the Problem-Solving Two Step: the participants' needs (see pages 36-37). Identification of needs is not always easy. It can take time for the shift from demands to needs to come into focus. You need to be sensitive to how the conflict may have impacted the ability of the participants to meet their needs, not only their substantive transactional needs, but also their identity, relationship and process needs.

Process overview

Your first consideration is whether to start with a caucus. Please review the guidance provided for this in Chapter 11.

Assuming you do not start with a caucus (but if you do, then after the caucus), begin by sharing the perspective of the participant who was identified to go first during the opening phase. You should demonstrate understanding through reflective listening. Making a summary is a good way to do this. Summarize the proceedings when you feel it is necessary, at any time during the process.

To get things started, you may say: *"OK, now that we are ready to get started, I am going to turn to you Sally, and ask that you share your perspective of the situation. What has happened, and how do you feel about it? I will be listening and will summarize my understanding of the gist of what you say first, before I turn to Harry."*

Welcome the opportunity to listen to, and summarize your understanding of, the second participant (Harry) before he begins. You should also 'clear the table' to ensure that he has the opportunity to share as if he had gone first. Harry should not feel the compulsion to rebut.

"Thanks for waiting, Harry. Now it is your turn to share your perspective. I want you to feel free to express yourself in the manner

that makes sense to you. Although you may be tempted to respond to what Sally said, only do so if it makes sense to you. I am going to listen to you, just the way I did with Sally."

Exactly how you support the participants' conversation will vary. Sometimes, you will need to spend more time with one participant because that person has more issues they want to address. At other times, based on the opening statements, you will develop an agenda and discuss the issues one at a time.

Especially where there are disputes, it makes sense to fragment the conflict by breaking it down into manageable, bite-sized components which we call 'the issues'. Mediators identify and carefully frame all the issues in the most conciliatory manner possible. They then structure the rest of the mediation session around this list of issues.

"I noticed that each of you have a number of issues you would like to address. I wonder if it would make sense to identify them in a list, and then talk about them one at a time?"

You may think it necessary to fully clarify one participant's perspective first. However, the danger of this approach is that the other 'listening' participant might lose patience and become agitated, especially if what is being said is difficult for that person to hear. In this case, it would be better to let them take turns.

A good general intervention is to make writing materials available to the participants. This gives the one something to do while the other is speaking. Tell them that if they are afraid of forgetting their questions or points of concern while the other is speaking, they should rather make notes than interrupt.

As mentioned, the sharing of perspectives is typically accomplished by each participant taking a turn to talk without being interrupted. For example, Sally may start with an opening statement, and Harry would follow with his. This would then be followed by another structured set of turns. After this it may become more erratic. You should also expect to encounter an interruption.

Once you are aware of an interruption, you are at a choice point and need to decide how to intervene. You can do nothing or you can do something – both are interventions. Expect the possibility that the intervention you choose may not have a positive impact. Be open to feedback at all times, and adjust your interventions accordingly.

"I noticed another interruption. I do not want to stifle the conversation, but I do want to make sure we all understand each other clearly."

Sometimes, all it takes is a look for there to be acknowledgement and change. Remember, it is generally hard for the participants to fundamentally change their communication dynamics.

Be careful of stifling a conversation by being too strict. Some of the conflict should be allowed into the room. You want the participants to be real with one another. Ultimately, you want to allow the freedom of open expression, as long as it is productive and in the spirit of the agreed-upon ground rules. When trust levels are low, you will need to be more vigilant about the enforcement of ground rules.

There will be times when the situation demands that you stay on top of things and enforce the ground rules more assertively. The communication may break down due to interruptions. Interrupting may be the dysfunctional style of communication used by the participants. Be sensitive of existing cultural norms, and coach them regarding effective communication techniques. Be careful, as how you handle these first infractions will be closely monitored. Whatever the infraction, a basic technique is to review procedural agreements. Mostly, this is all that is needed to regain their commitment.

"Allowing the speaker to finish what s/he is saying was agreed upon up front when we established ground rules. We can talk about this if we need to. The last thing I want to do is impede your conversation. However, in my experience I have found that the process works better when each person is at ease, knowing there is space to finish. Do we need to talk about this?"

A more directive intervention to the challenge of interruptions is: *"Let's talk about interruptions now, before we get back to sharing about the issues. It is important that we are all on the same page."*

The conversation may feel a little awkward and even stilted in the beginning but will flow more naturally after a while. If the participants are conversing about the issues at stake in a generally productive manner, relax. This signifies that there is some momentum and that they are making progress. Remain present and engaged in the conversation, always ready to respond with a different intervention based on your ongoing openness to feedback.

What happened: their observations as facts

As the participants share their observations, and educate one another about how they see the situation, it is inevitable that they will reveal their version of what happened. In other words, they will share their perspective using their 'facts' based on their memories. How you manage this is vital. Mediation is not a fact-finding process, and so while it is one thing to share the facts, it is another thing to make definitive determinations on these facts. You want to make it clear from the start, and reiterate often, that you are not a judge, an arbitrator, or an investigator. As mediator, your role is not to adjudicate but to hold the space for the reality of the two perspectives.

Avoid the use of the word 'story' to frame the participants' relationship to what happened. It suggests something has been made up. The word 'perspective' does not have this connotation. Everyone has a perspective. So, rather than asking them to 'tell their side of the story', which sets up an adversarial dynamic, use inclusive language and frame the challenge mutually.

*"You will each have an opportunity to share your **perspective** of the situation and educate one another on how best to move forward."*

Despite the use of the word 'perspective' (or another similar word) to frame and also influence how each participant shares, expect accusations of dishonesty and lying. It takes great tact to maintain your balance while addressing these concerns.

*"My sense is that, while there is a lot that you agree upon, there are also areas where you disagree. Rather than getting caught in a 'he said, she said' conversation, accept that you are not going to agree about certain things. As I have explained, mediation is not a fact-finding process. And we do not have to resolve these different perceptions of the facts in order for you to work something out. Actually, mediation is a wonderful process which allows you to explore **how** you see things differently, and to see what shifts both of you can make in this regard."*

The basis for your approach to the two different perspectives is to understand that memory is limited, especially when you take into account the fallibility of cognition. You need to normalize the reality that the two participants will have different memories and therefore different perspectives. Do not be bothered by this fact. Your role is to meet the participants with their perspectives. They may shift their perception of the 'facts', and if they do, the resolution of the conflict will be all the more profound. But they may not. And if they do not, whether in full or in part, you should remind them that this is *not* a reason for not working something out.

"This process focuses on creatively addressing both your needs. I am not your judge. I will not resolve any 'factual' disputes. And, in fact, you do not need to either. You may never be able to convince one another that your respective version of the facts is correct. However, that is not a reason for you failing to come to an agreement. As long as we can identify your needs, we can find a solution."

The danger of retelling is that the neural pathways are strengthened with each rendition. Grant the past a limited role and honor that. Intervene when you have a sense that the participants are repeating themselves like a stuck record. One way to approach the retelling of a perspective is to ensure that you have listened deeply and have summarized what has been said, felt and thought.

Another way to respond would be to use the technique called 'the loop of understanding', which is very powerful. You will need the co-operation of both participants for this to work. It is ideal when you have a sense that being heard would satisfy one or both of the participants. By the time you use this technique, you should have role-modeled active listening and the summarizing of what each person has said. You should also have set it up so that each participant is taking a turn to speak and listen.

Here is how the loop of understanding technique works: *"My sense is that it would be helpful for you both to have the benefit of being heard by the other. Here is what I am going to ask you to do. Bill, you can go first. Tell Dennis what you want him to understand from your perspective."* Then, immediately turn to Dennis and say: *"Dennis, I want you to listen to what Bill says. Allow him to finish, then summarize your understanding of what he just said. If you can reflect back how he feels, so much the better. After you have satisfied Bill that you have heard him, though not necessarily agreed with him, it will be your turn."* End by asking: *"What questions do you have?"* This form is generally better than asking them whether they have any questions, which makes it too easy for them to say 'no'.

Creating the safe space for both perspectives to be held as valid is a vital function of the mediator. You are not agreeing with the participants; rather, you are showing them that you understand how they see things. This is the heart of validation and the education phase.

Mediation has a future focus. The facts are from the past and, as you have pointed out to the participants, dependent on our fallible memories. The danger of trying to get all factual disputes resolved is that you get stuck there. Generally, a past focus is justified only to the extent that it informs the participants about what they need to do differently when moving forward. If you have a background in adjudication, especially if you have undertaken employee investigations, making the necessary shift away from a factual focus can be difficult.

What they feel: their emotions

Given the centrality of emotions to the conflict-resolution process, it follows that this is one of the most important conversations for you to facilitate. Remember, there are two conversations about emotions. The one is about the conflict itself. The other is about the feelings that are being generated by the mediation process. Obviously they are connected, but it is helpful to make the distinction. For example, a participant may express anger about what happened but be satisfied with the way the mediation process is going.

As regards the conflict itself, support the participants to identify and express how they felt in an appropriate manner. We socialize one another to not trust our feelings. We are told to be happy when we are sad; content when we are angry. As a result, many participants will be disconnected from what they really feel and afraid of opening the pro-verbial can of worms to discover these true feelings. Others will have a sense of what they feel and be able to verbalize this. The participants will probably assume responsibility to differing degrees, based on their maturity and self-awareness.

Always meet the participants where they are at. To do this, you need to tune into and get a sense of the intensity of their emotional states. When you summarize, as you need to do throughout a mediation, look for ways of surfacing what you have sensed about their emotions. In all your efforts, remain mindful of the safety needs of the participants and also of their cultural norms as regards expressing emotionality. Consider doing some of this work through private caucuses.

For example, imagine you are mediating with three laborers for a local utility company. Two have sided against one. The excluded person is at breaking point. You sense his need to emote as he is getting in touch with his pain. You also see his white knuckles, and understand that he thinks he has to muscle his way through in order to save face.

At this point, you could try to diffuse the situation by saying: *"I was thinking that now would be a good time to caucus. I would like to meet with each of you in private. Remember, what each of you says will be kept in confidence and I will only repeat what you instruct me to."*

The caucus is a powerful tool. It is well suited for a private conversation about feelings. Regardless of whether you are in a caucus or not, use your own knowledge of the different emotional signatures, including the non-verbal ones, to see if you can sense the core feelings that are feeding the conflict. Sometimes, the participants may use words which indicate their emotions, but often you will have to get the ball rolling.

Anger is often the presenting emotion that masks the pain of sadness, fear, jealousy, and shame. Be gentle when you suggest something. It can be with words, such as: *"I imagine you are worried about your job."* In that short sentence, you have suggested both the feeling and its intensity. Hopefully, your acknowledgement is accurate and you are in the ballpark. If you are not, you will probably be told so.

Be careful to monitor for the participants' acceptance of your sense of the emotions at play. You should never second guess them. If needs be, apologize if one of them says something like: "No, actually, I am not feeling worried. It is something else." Honor the feedback non-defensively and then respond differently, based on your new awareness. The net result is that a conversation has been started which, at its conclusion, will hopefully have identified to the participants' satisfaction what and how strongly they felt. You may hear words to this effect: "Actually, when I think about it, I feel disappointed.

We were buddies. I had trusted that he would look out for me and he did not."

Beyond helping the participants to identify the full range of their feelings in relation to what happened, be alert to the possibility that either one or both of them may be open to exploring the more inner conflict-resolution paths, even forgiveness. It can start very innocently. One of the participants may say something vulnerable, such as: "You know, I wonder about this disappointment thing that is going on." This would be an opportunity for the deeper conversation that allows the participants to see how the energy of the conflict is sourced from within, and how it continues to influence the thought patterns that hold the conflict in place.

One possible way of responding to this would be to have the conversation in private. However, if the participant is able to talk openly with the other present, imagine how powerful that could be. For example, you could say: *"Are you willing to say more? If both of you can get to the emotions that are holding your conflict in place, so much the better. Often, manifested conflict is a reflection of unresolved energy within us. Do you have a sense of what is going on with this disappointment? When else have you experienced this? What is your earliest memory of something like this?"*

Allow the participant to share this kind of delicate information in a way that makes sense to the person. You may hear words to this effect: "It always comes up. I trust someone and then they let me down. This is not the first time I have had this kind of experience." Give the participants space to connect with what they are now eventually feeling. Often, they are figuring it out for the first time. Listen for the metaphors they use and try to connect as closely as you can with their experience.

At some point, one of the participants may make a conciliatory gesture. In the extreme, this would be an unconditional apology, with a sincere expression of remorse, an undertaking to correct the situation, and a promise never to do it again. When this happens, do not be surprised to see significant shifts. As Daniel Dana, a pioneering author of managerial mediation has helped us to understand, conciliatory gestures invoke the inhibitory reflex, which makes it very difficult for us to be anything but conciliatory in return.[1]

However, most of the time, the conciliatory gesture will not be as grand as that stated above. It is more likely to be expressed by a resigned or sad look that indicates an apology, or a statement that indicates a shift. For example, a participant may say: "When we started, I thought I had no part in this. But now I am starting to see that I have some responsibility."

The danger is that a vulnerable gesture like this can be lost in the turmoil of a conversation. Imagine, for example, that on hearing something like the above, the other participant says, sarcastically: "Damn right you are responsible! That is what I have been saying all along. It amazes me that you took so long to figure it out!" When this happens, instead of the gesture being converted into trust, the opposite occurs. The vulnerable participant concludes that it is now unsafe to participate and becomes angry that the gesture was not appreciated. Be ready to intervene before any damage is done.

Your ability to 'sit in the fire' during the expression of strong emotions will encourage the participants to do the same. If you are uncomfortable, the participants will feel it. Do not minimize or stifle emotional expression. Rather, seek to normalize it by commenting directly when the emotion surfaces, such as: *"It is normal to be angry when this happens."* Be careful not to set yourself up with statements that will be difficult to defend, such as: *"I know just how you feel."* Or: *"I understand."*

Do not be afraid to use humor, and get everyone laughing together. Be welcoming and hospitable. Look for small opportunities for collaboration and build on them. Reinforce positive moves and remain in a good mood throughout.

Sometimes, grief or other strong emotions are best expressed in private. Give the participants options, such as: *"Are you comfortable discussing this in the joint session? Would you prefer to talk privately?"*

It is only a question of time before someone cries during one of your mediations. Tears are typically a sign that emotional pain and discomfort are being addressed; that a thawing or healing is taking place. If people are to move beyond their anger, grief or fear, they must feel it. Validate the tears, in other words, let the person know that their emotional response is a valid one.

Given that crying can constitute a loss of face for some people, and that they may prefer the opportunity to cry in private, it is wise to check in and get a sense of what is needed. If necessary, meet with the participant who is crying in private. However, beware of ushering the person away and thus sending a wrong message that tears are negative.

In anticipation of possible tears, have handkerchiefs available on or near the table, but do not offer one as your first response when someone cries, as this may imply that crying is inappropriate. Worse still, it may take the person away from what they are feeling.

Beyond the more intuitive reasons to value tears, it is interesting to know that, from a physiological point of view, tears are a way for the body to release stress-related hormones, like cortisol. Tears are a source of information and an opportunity to address the emotional energy of the conflict. Be sensitive, and work to validate the emotions associated with the tears. It could be the very thing that helps the participants to reach a lasting resolution.

Another related procedural path is to explore how each participant reacts behaviorally when emotionally triggered. It is one thing to feel those old, unresolved feelings so that you slowly but surely reduce the emotional charge you are carrying. It is another thing to change the way you react from a protective to a non-defensive pattern when you are triggered.

When the participants are in ongoing relationships, they will both need to address this important aspect of relational life: how to relate when one or both of them are upset. For the one, the challenge may be anger management, while for the other it may be the lack of awareness regarding passive-aggressive behavior. Owning these as their patterns is the first step; changing their behaviors is the second. Both steps are challenging, and thanks to the plasticity of the brain, both are possible. When we normalize this as both a shared human challenge and an opportunity, the relief can be palpable.

Your attitude towards the expression of emotion is all-important. Emotions are part of being human. We cannot be anything but emotional, even when we try not to be. We connect through our contagious emotions. And discover that emotions are the gateway to deeper levels of resolution.

What they think: their assumptions

As mediator, your task is to work with the assumptions the participants make about each other's motives, as well as those they make about the 'facts'. Typically, both participants will have formed negative impressions of one another, in particular their motives, which they will most likely perceive as hostile and interfering. Furthermore, all the information that makes it through to their conscious minds is being filtered through a lens that is predisposed to see scarcity and incompatibility.

Making assumptions is normal. Your challenge is to make explicit those assumptions that are getting in the way of productive problem solving. Unless you are dealing with very self-aware participants, they will most likely be blind to the fact that they are seeing and hearing what they expect to see and hear. As a result, you should approach the exploration of assumptions with great tact.

The best way to do this is to normalize the fact that we all make different assumptions based on our perceptions. You should validate the participants' individual perceptions extensively. In other words, allow the different perspectives that you are told to coexist. Your ability to hold both realities will create the trusting, safe environment necessary for you to ask questions.

In a joint session, you may say something like this: *"You mentioned that you did not trust Sally. I understand that you felt let down and were embarrassed that you only found out about X at the meeting. But I am wondering whether the belief that Sally is untrustworthy is the only conclusion possible."*

You may want to explain fundamental attribution error, which refers to the way we tend to attribute excusable environmental factors to our own failings, while we attribute personality flaws to the failings of others. You could ask: *"Could that be going on here? I do not know, but would like you to look at it."* Try to normalize the fact that unless we are careful, we tend to jump to conclusions about the personality or ability of other people, which reflects double standards.

Often this will lead to a chuckle, and you are on your way. Do not try to force participants to see things. Be respectful of their intelligence. If your suggestion does not resonate, move on. Find a new way to intervene.

Helping both participants to understand how easy it is to attribute a negative motive or intention to the other, especially when the impact has been painful, can help to normalize this behavior. Questions that are combined with statements of observation are effective in exploring the validity of perceptions. For instance: *"You said that your supervisor does not care about you. What led you to that conclusion? Is it possible that there are things you do not know about?"*

This could lead to a fruitful conversation about assumptions regarding managerial responsibility. It may lead to the realization that the supervisor does a lot of the things associated with care. As suggested earlier, sometimes it is wise to let the participants agree to disagree. This is helpful where the issue in dispute does not have to be decided in order for a resolution to emerge: *"It seems as if you see this differently. However, that should not get in the way of you working something out today."*

Probably the most important assumptions to explore are the participants' expectations of what will happen if they do not reach a resolution. What are their alternatives to resolution? It is unwise to address this too early on in the mediation. I explore this further in Chapter 9, in the discussion on the negotiation phase.

What they want: their needs

The key to solving a conflict is the identification of the participants' underlying needs. One of the most important tasks of the mediator is to make these needs explicit. The participants typically come to the mediation aware of what they want (their ideal solution), but few have done the preparation work that helps them to discover why they want this particular outcome (their needs).

One of the most fundamental reframes in mediation is from demands to needs. Use every chance to do this. Reframe: *"We cannot keep on having these dysfunctional dynamics."* to *"You need reliable staff who do what they commit to, and who communicate when there is a problem."*

It takes practice reframing to needs. You will find a needs inventory included as Appendix 3 on page 163, which contains a list of words that are helpful to use when identifying and framing needs.

When there is no new information surfacing and the participants have cleared the air and discharged enough of the emotional charge to start problem solving, start steering the conversation towards the listing of needs.

"Sounds like we are ready to clarify your needs. I am going to record them on this chart here. I have drawn a T-bar. On the left-hand side I have written Sally's name. I am going to record all her needs beneath her name. Then I will do the same for you, Harry. In fact, we can all do this together. Our goal is to make sure that we have a comprehensive overview of all your needs."

In some situations, you may choose to record the participants' needs on a chart or whiteboard. Use the T-bar from Step One of the Problem-Solving Two Step (see page 36). In other situations, you may prefer to keep track of the participants' respective needs mentally, or on a note pad. Or you could use a computer with a projector or screen. Whichever way you choose to do this, articulate the participants' needs back to them and ensure that you gain confirmation that you have understood them correctly. Always be ready to give a global summary of their needs.

Needs	
Sally	Harry
• Job security	• Job security
• Good reputation with management	• Good reputation with supervisors
• Fairness	• Performance
• Opportunity	• Reliability
• Understanding	• Accountability
• Change	• Change
• Respect	• Respect
• Professionalism	• Professionalism

"You both value your jobs and are concerned that this conflict will reflect poorly to your supervisors. You want to work something out that feels fair. Sally, you considered your most recent performance review to be unfair, and have concerns about how it will impact your career. Harry, you need to know that when a scheduled one-on-one meeting is missed, a new meeting date will be made. You were

frustrated at what you perceived to be a pattern of forgetfulness, and wanted to draw Sally's attention to this in a very clear manner. Your challenge is to find a solution that addresses these needs in the most creative manner possible. Oh, and I heard you both saying you wanted a respectful and professional relationship."

You should be able to get a good sense of what the participants need by listening to them with needs identification in mind. It may be helpful to ask questions to focus the conversation on needs: *"What do you need?"* or *"What are you concerned about?"* or *"What is important to you?"*

The question 'why?' is extremely powerful and will help the participants to articulate their needs: *"You said that keeping your employment with the company is important. Can you say why?"*

Remember to explore the full spectrum of the participants' needs. Their relational and identity needs are particularly important in ongoing relationships. Belonging, being valued, being treated with respect, and being supported in order to be successful are important relationship needs. Being seen as competent, fair and intelligent are typical identity needs.

Transitioning to the option-generation phase

Do not become stuck in the past. The relevance of the past, in the context of mediation, is to discover and most creatively address both participants' needs in moving forward. Mediation has a future focus, and while the education phase involves looking into the past, it does so to learn how best to approach the future. A focus on dynamics rather than details is often helpful.

When you have a good sense of the participants' respective needs and how they prioritize them, you are ready to initiate the option-generation phase.

"You both have valid needs. The challenge is to find solutions that address all of them. This is the work of the option-generation phase, to which we can now move."

---

[1] Dana, 1999.

Chapter 8

The Option-Generation Phase

*"Participants develop a list of possible options to
deal with the issue. Process is creative, imaginative,
free-flowing, with deferred reactions/judgments."*

Mark Bennett and Michele Hermann

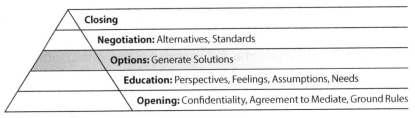

The Mediation Process

During option-generation, the participants work together to develop a range of possible solutions that address all the needs they identified during the education phase. This phase represents the second step of the Problem-Solving Two Step. As the quote above suggests, participants need to be at their creative best. They most commonly brainstorm, either formally or informally, to generate solutions.

Sometimes, participants come across a unique solution that no one has thought of before. Generally, there is a range to what is possible in the circumstances. As mediator, your awareness of what others have done in similar situations is invaluable. You may at times suggest ('float') tried and tested solutions for the participants to consider. Remember, your role is to *not* decide for them.

In many situations, the participants will want to see common elements addressed. Guide them to explore not only these elements but also the unexpected avenues, which can often present surprising results.

The greatest challenge is to complete the work of the education phase. Although the participants are naturally eager to explore potential solutions, they risk setbacks if they do not first attend to the tasks of the education phase.

Process overview

In a very real sense, the participants are limited by their own creativity. To be creative, and to have the agility necessary to find the best possible solution, they should be emotionally composed and, ideally, experiencing feelings of satisfaction, happiness and joy. Yet this is often not the case. As mediator, you need to meet them where they are, not where you would like them to be. Even though the ideal is not always the case, at the very least the participants should feel that they have been heard and understood. There should be a sense of satisfaction that progress is being made.

Also, there should be an ongoing sense of safety, no matter how bruising the revelations of the education phase may have been. Hopefully, the participants will also see that despite the exploration of a difficult and painful matter, the conversation was focused, productive, and conducted with an acceptable degree of composure. At this point, you should be an inspiring 'cheerleader', encouraging them and pointing to their accomplishments. Sincere and believable expressions of optimism are always helpful.

"It always takes time to do the work of the education phase. I was impressed by the way you both shared your perspectives with one another. It was not easy at times, but you pulled through. Now you have a wonderful opportunity to use the information you learnt, especially about each other's needs, to explore what is possible."

It is important to underscore the fact that the participants are not agreeing to anything at this point. This, more than anything, puts them at ease.

"I want to be very clear. The ideas you throw out are only possible solutions. You saying 'terminate' or 'promote' as ideas to resolve the conflict does not mean that you have agreed to either of them. We will, in a very focused manner, review the ideas you brainstorm and use them to negotiate the final terms, to which you will both agree."

When we brainstorm in a mediation, we separate the generation of ideas from the evaluation of ideas, in other words, we separate the development of options from the choice of particular solutions. This approach prevents the participants from attaching to particular solutions, or reverting to their pre-mediation positions. How carefully you calibrate the brainstorming session can make a world of difference.

"I imagine both of you know what brainstorming means. I often comment that we all know what it is and we all struggle with it. We know we should not criticize or judge ideas. Yet you may ask yourself why you should keep quiet if, for instance, you know there is no money in the budget for an idea that is being suggested. The reason to not criticize or judge ideas is because that stifles creativity. So, rule number one is no criticism, and that is not limited to verbal criticism. Rule number two is quantity is more important than quality in this instance, so all ideas are welcome. This specifically includes wild and crazy notions that may be surprising.

"As you share ideas, you may be tempted to piggyback off something one of you has said. The variety that emerges from doing this is great. Therefore, please do piggyback.

"I may join in if I am aware of a solution that others have used in similar circumstances. As mediators, we say we are 'floating solutions'. The fact that I mention something does not mean you should agree to it. Consider it to be just another possible solution for you both to consider.

"Finally, it helps if you think outside the box and do not assume that there is one single or right solution to the problem. In the same way, assuming that there is a 'fixed pie' is counterproductive."

As mediator, you will need to work hard to create an environment in which the participants feel safe to collaborate rather than compete. When they know that all ideas are welcome, they usually relax into the process and see things that they would not necessarily have seen before. When they hear their 'opponent' suggest an idea that addresses their needs, they are often motivated to reciprocate.

Be careful not to neglect the needs that have been articulated by the participants. Before moving on from brainstorming, it is important that you support them to reconcile their options with their prioritized needs. Ensure that they have developed options that address *all* of their identified needs.

Apart from this more formal brainstorming, facilitate the development of options informally through open discussion. Participants should throw out ideas or scenarios and ask themselves whether they would work. People feel safe doing this when they know their ideas are not binding. You are there to ensure that they keep to the point when addressing identified issues. You should also be ready to provide ongoing summaries of emerging areas of agreement and disagreement should they be needed.

Although ideally there should be no evaluation of the ideas at this point, realistically this is unlikely, and the participants will probably engage in some analysis. Monitor the mood closely. The last thing you want to do is stifle productive work.

In general, making information about the negotiation process graphically available is a powerful yet simple intervention. The Problem-Solving Two Step lends itself to being recorded. I encourage the use of visual recording tools, such as flip charts, whiteboards, or computer-generated projections. Being able to see something graphically provides encouragement and stimulates creativity.

Computers lend themselves to the use of precedents and what is referred to as 'single-text negotiation', that is, once the potential solutions have been identified, the mediator drafts a document that records the points on which agreement has been reached. This text then becomes the point of reference/departure for the finalization of the agreement. To help you draft a simple settlement agreement, I have included a sample document as Appendix 5 on page 167. This is based on the mediation we will conduct between Harry and Sally in Chapter 12, with clauses that you can modify for your own use.

Standard solutions for perception of hurt

People in conflict who believe they have been hurt usually expect solutions that address their need for:

- **information** about what happened
- **acknowledgement** of how they felt
- **reparations** (restoration, or being 'made whole' again)
- **learning** (reassurance that what happened is unlikely to recur).

By exploring the importance of these four need categories during the education phase, the mediator sets up the participants to expand their solution 'pie' during the option-generation phase.

Let us take a look at these need categories one at a time.

Information

"I do not understand why..." is a phrase you may hear the reprimanded participant ask early on in the proceedings. Not knowing is unsettling, and often the simple fact of knowing what happened and why has tremendous value. Therefore, there is a real need for the sharing of information, especially in the context of performance management. Bear in mind that a lot of information will be shared naturally during the education phase.

Participants may not like or agree with what they hear when information is shared. They may be embarrassed, dispute the relevance of the information, or question the conclusions drawn. For example, when a participant has not been given any ongoing feedback about performance issues but receives a poor formal review, s/he may want to know what information was used for the review, and may ask for timely information in future so as to improve. The kind of information needed may be the results of an investigation or report, or a medical test that one or the other wants. It is not unusual to hear requests for information about what other people are being paid, or about their disciplinary record. Sometimes, the need is to protect information rather than to share it. Be sensitive regarding all these possibilities.

When the information sought is not immediately available, agreeing to provide it as and when it becomes available is often a sensible solution. Making commitments about how vital information is shared in the future is more procedural, but still attends to the need for information.

While the mediation may result in the surfacing of conflicts that are sourced from a lack of information, or misinformation, or questions about relevance, the mediation is not the appropriate forum to resolve these conflicts on the participants' behalf.

"As you know, mediation is not a fact-finding process. As a result, I cannot resolve this difference over the relevance or accuracy of

the information. The forum to do that is a court of law, and you are always at liberty to make that choice. Or you can work with what you have, despite the uncertainty. Many disputants do. They are able to focus on what they need, and let go of being factually right."

The participants will come to their own respective conclusions about the information. As I have stated previously, they do not have to see things the same way. They can agree to disagree about the past, and agree to agree about the future they want to create together.

Legal information often plays a role in the resolution of workplace disputes. Where you anticipate that this will be the case, it is important to ensure that the participants establish protocols for examining such data. Avoiding a discussion about the legal ramifications is not wise, especially where the participants believe the law is on their side.

It is not unusual for the participants to have different ideas about what information is needed, or how it should be interpreted. Increasingly, employees turn to the internet for information about their employment rights. Figuring out what is credible and what is misleading is a delicate task. Warn them not to make assumptions, as these are often false and can cause them to interpret data in a way that is consistent with their assumptions rather than with the truth.

Reaching agreement on what information is needed, and then agreeing on a process to collect that information, helps to reframe the conflict in a problem-solving manner. Ideally, information gathering should be a shared task. Rather than each participant developing an independent set of data, strive for a common database. It may be useful to obtain the opinions of other people with expertise who are credible to the participants. They can be helpful in interpreting the information from another perspective.

Acknowledgement

The acknowledgement of our experience, especially when it is difficult, is often the key to moving forward. Until the pain has been acknowledged to their satisfaction, the participants are often stuck. As a general rule, acknowledgements made by the participants to one another are more powerful and effective than the mediator's acknowledgements.

The shifts can be dramatic when participant acknowledgement occurs. A sincere apology, as an extreme example of an acknowledgement, can take the wind out of the most righteous of sails. Generally, acknowledgements occur organically within the mediation. However, exploring the specific need for a formal apology is often a good idea, even if it does not go anywhere.

When a participant can acknowledge being the stimulus for another's discomfort, pain, disappointment and even frustration, without justification or defensiveness, it is very hard to react harshly. In fact, as explained in the previous chapter, Daniel Dana asserts that conciliatory acknowledgements produce an inhibitory reflex.[1] Like dogs, when one assumes a submissive posture, the other backs off.

Take care to manage these interactions. They can easily lead to resentments and new feelings of abuse and exploitation if an apology is ignored or trashed. Remember that conciliatory gestures occur on a continuum and, if handled well, are likely to propel the participants towards resolution.

Reparations

Generally, when we apologize in a way that suggests that we assume responsibility, we offer to make the other participant 'whole'. Imagine your child has thrown a ball through your neighbor's window. You send him over to apologize. It is reasonable for your neighbor to expect that, in addition to the apology, there will be an undertaking on your part to repair the window.

However, a participant may acknowledge hurt feelings, and even that the other has been harmed, but not assume responsibility. "I am sorry you are in this position, but I am not responsible." The fear of being held responsible is the main reason people are unwilling to apologize. Of course, the question of responsibility will be one of the substantive issues that the mediation will address.

Navigating these conversations can be tricky. Sometimes, no apology is better than an insincere one. When a formal apology is to be given, help the participants to think carefully about who will deliver it, where it will be delivered, and to whom. There is a big difference between a public and a private apology.

In the context of reparations, the reality is that we often talk about money as the way to make amends. Yet payment of money is seldom expected in the context of informal, in-house mediations. However, where there are allegations of discrimination or harassment, participants will often have expectations that they be paid something.

When the employer concludes that there has been no breach of the law, they will sometimes reluctantly pay what is referred to as 'nuisance value'. This is normally a nominal amount, anywhere from a few hundred dollars to fifty thousand dollars, to make the issue go away. Bear in mind that most people are uncomfortable talking about money. However, if money is an issue, make sure that the participants address it, whether or not any payment is made.

Learning

Beyond acknowledgement and reparations, there is the expectation that we will learn from our mistakes and not repeat the same hurtful behavior again.

"During the education phase, we established that there was a need to learn from this experience and do things differently in the future. I wonder what your ideas are for doing that?"

In essence, this is the reframe of the 'blame' conversation. As we support the participants to explore their respective responsibilities for the 'challenging situation', we encourage them to look at their contributions non-defensively in order to find creative solutions. Sensible solutions that address the challenge of how to avoid the conflict in future can be highly rewarding and creatively engaging.

Sometimes, solutions focus on shifting the culture system-wide, as when an organization seeks to move from a blame to a learning culture. This kind of shift usually has noble intentions and is a positive outcome. Often, the mediation highlights skills deficiencies that can be appropriately addressed through individual or group coaching or training.

Workplace issues: sample solutions

You, as mediator, are a source of ideas for potential solutions. This can be very helpful to the participants, as the same solutions come up again and again. Remember that when you float a solution, all you are doing is inviting the participants to consider it as a possibility.

Discipline

When the dispute centers on disciplinary action, differing perceptions and interpretations regarding what happened (the 'facts') will determine the kinds of solutions the participants will come up with. Here are some possibilities (bear in mind they disregard policy implications – we are brainstorming here, after all!):

Rescission or reduction in the severity of the penalty is always a possibility. Sometimes, the mediation brings new information to light that alters the perspective of what happened. At other times, a participant may demonstrate a learning mindset, and take responsibility.

Changing a termination of employment to a voluntary resignation will often be very valuable for an employee who needs to continue working. If this solution is proposed, flesh it out. For instance, consider who will handle the reference checks for this employee. There should be clarity regarding what can be said and by whom when the employee is recommended to a potential employer. You should aim to prevent surprises in the future.

Employees are often keen to have the disciplinary action removed from their personnel files and may suggest this be conditional on their future good conduct. If this is not permitted as a matter of policy or law, the employer may consider a 'positive' letter in the employee's file, to balance things out.

Performance

Performance issues are common, challenging, and not always easy to resolve. Money and job security are both linked to performance. These conversations often involve differences of perception regarding the accuracy of the information or the conclusion reached. Try to support the participants to reach sensible solutions.

While reassignment remains an option, especially in large organizations where it is possible to move employees around, it sometimes represents a lack of creativity in finding a better solution. Voluntary demotion is related to reassignment. Although a tough solution to agree upon, it may represent a better option than the alternative of termination.

Negotiating a performance improvement plan is often a sensible solution. The expectations that are conveyed to employees from management should always be clear. Establishing specific, measureable and attainable goals helps everyone. Training is also an ever-present option in the context of performance and is often highly valued as it signals a willingness to invest in the future together.

Treatment

How we treat one another matters. In the United States, federal and state laws prohibit discrimination and harassment on a variety of grounds including race, gender, ability, age and national origin.

Defensiveness is likely in a mediation when the allegation is discrimination or harassment. The classic reframe is to treatment: *"I hear that you are upset about your treatment. Talking about that is crucial for you, right?"*

When any such allegation is made, the law dictates that a fact-finding investigation be conducted to determine the facts, apply them to the law, and come to a conclusion as to whether or not discrimination or harassment has occurred. Mediation is encouraged as an alternative; in fact, it is mandated as a choice for all federal employees in the United States. When an employee makes an allegation of discrimination, the choice of mediation is offered. Mediation either suspends the investigation track, or runs along a parallel track. In either case, the failure to work things out in mediation does not negate any of the employee's rights, and in these cases the investigation continues. Mediation is also offered after the conclusion of an investigation.

The harsh consequences of admitting intentional (and even negligent) discriminatory practices mean that they are almost never admitted to. However, this should not stop participants from agreeing to solutions that apparently address how they treat one another, despite their possible refusal to admit guilt. On the rare occasions when there is an admission of discrimination or harassment, the solution will most likely include an apology.

Reassignment is common in the context of discrimination or harassment cases, especially during the course of an investigation. When the reassignment is temporary, helping the two employees involved to work together can be challenging. In these cases, post-investigation mediation can be especially helpful. Sometimes, the reassignment becomes permanent.

Sensitivity and other soft-skills training, such as conflict resolution and emotional intelligence, are other common solutions. More and more, coaching is used rather than sending an employee to training.

Promotions

Conflict over promotions is common. Employees sometimes believe that they are entitled to a promotion, or feel that another person's promotion is unfair. When a peer becomes a boss as a result of a promotion, relationships can often become strained.

As with disciplinary issues, sometimes information comes to light that leads to the granting of a promotion. When this easy solution does not magically appear, consider suggesting placement the next time a vacancy becomes available, or at least notification and prioritization in respect of all new vacancies.

It can be helpful to clarify company policy and expectations with regard to promotions. Related solutions can focus on addressing the ability gap that is impeding an expected promotion. Other possibilities include coaching, training in relevant skills, and studying further.

Relational solutions

In addition to the above-mentioned possible solutions for typical workplace issues, your experience in supporting healthy and productive relationships can lead to the mention of a variety of very different kinds of solutions.

"You have both indicated that you want to restore a professional working relationship that is characterized by open communication. I wonder what ideas you have that would support this?"

The use of context-setting background recitals to contextualize a conflict often serves to underscore the participants' commitment to a professional working relationship. In addition, establishing open and clear communication is vital when the relationship is ongoing. Solutions should specifically address when and how feedback is given, and clarify different roles.

Where the participants have opened up to each other and revealed information about their emotional intelligence, in particular the things that trigger them and how they calm down, the opportunity presents itself to guide them to find ways to deal with these important topics.

"I commend you both for the way you opened up and shared. It is often comforting to discover that we all struggle with reactive tendencies. Knowing what our 'hot buttons' are can be helpful, so we do not keep throwing unnecessary salt on the wound. Knowing how to support one another to calm down is also a good idea. What are your thoughts about including some of this in your agreement?"

'Time out' clauses are another common solution to relational aspects of a dispute that find their way into agreements. These clauses essentially allow the participants to ask for a break in the conversation ('time out') and take responsibility for reconvening the postponed conversation in the near future.

"Participants sometimes like a 'time out' clause, which means that either of you can signal, in a pre-determined manner, that now is not a good time to continue the conversation. If you opt for this, you are responsible for reconvening the conversation within an agreed-upon period of time. Is this something that would make sense? If so, how would you like to customize it?"

Suggest that the participants check in with each other at various intervals and at a venue that is perhaps more socially relaxed. They will ultimately decide what they want to do. Acknowledge their willingness to work on the relationship.

"I am encouraged that you both want to turn the corner and restore a productive relationship. Investing in the relationship will help. I heard one of you mention the possibility of having regular

check-ins. This is a popular solution that demonstrates an earnest desire to make it work. It allows you to clear any misunderstanding early. Would you like to explore this some more?"

When participants are concerned about what to say to others when the mediation is over, you may invite the consideration of a 'press release' clause. This clarifies for everyone what they will say if they are asked. Usually, participants agree to say something like: "Yes, we mediated and worked something out. Thanks for asking. I am not at liberty to say more."

"No doubt, some of your colleagues know you are in a mediation. What are you going to tell them when it is over? One possibility is to include what I call a 'press release' clause in your agreement, which will state your agreement regarding what you will both say if you are asked about the mediation."

Realistically, it will take time to steer a relational conflict in a more productive direction. The more emotional energy felt and integrated by both participants, the better. Encouraging them to revise their expectations about one another will help them to prepare for the new behavioral norms that will be embodied in the ultimate agreement.

You can support the participants to keep to their agreements in a number of ways. Firstly, document exactly what is agreed upon. Secondly, suggest a 'dispute-resolution' clause to serve as a reminder to everyone that conflict is normal, and that anticipating this fact represents the wise approach. Thirdly, express a desire for mediator follow-up. Your desire and intention to follow up is important. This is one of the key ways you signal care, and contracts with the participants to hold them accountable for keeping to the new terms of their agreement.

"Reaching agreements is hard work. But the hardest work is sticking to them. Habits are difficult to change, and things may happen that will tempt you to assign a negative intention to each other's behavior. It helps to know exactly what you will do if you have a future disagreement. Firstly, know that this is normal. Secondly, it is wise to address concerns as soon as possible. In addition, I encourage you to allow me to follow up with you in about sixty days, to see how things are going. Participants usually find that this arrangement motivates them to keep to the new agreements."

Transitioning to the negotiation phase

Realistically, participants will struggle to stay in a purely brainstorming mode. Some evaluations are inevitable, especially when you generate ideas in an open discussion. However, quantity trumps quality in this context, and the more possible ideas you can get out into the open before the participants start to evaluate and negotiate, the better.

"You have both done a great job brainstorming potential solutions that satisfy the needs we identified during the education phase. As we move to consider which you are going to agree upon, I think you will see that the variety and creativity you have brought to the table have been most helpful. We will now turn to negotiation in order to determine what you are willing to agree upon."

---

[1]   Dana, 1999.

Chapter 9
The Negotiation Phase

"Mediation is assisted negotiation."

Jim Melamed

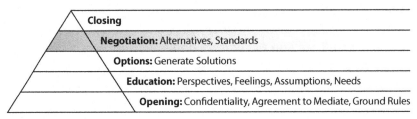

The Mediation Process

As the quote above suggests, when people attempt to resolve a conflict through negotiation and have chosen to mediate, in a very real sense the mediation process is an assisted negotiation.

During the negotiation phase, the participants jointly assess the potential solutions that have been generated during the option-generation phase and negotiate any settlement terms. This phase has much in common with the education phase in that the participants educate each other about how they feel, how well the potential solutions meet their needs, and what they perceive to be possible.

Negotiations are primarily a blend of both collaborative and competitive strategies. As mediator, you should be biased towards collaborative behavior. However, the reality is that many participants in a mediation are competitive, and almost all negotiations involve some elements of competition. This means that you need to be competent intervening with both competitive and collaborative negotiation styles.

Two conversations are central to any negotiation to deal with this tension between competition and collaboration. The first focuses on standards of fairness, the second on alternatives to agreement.

Regarding fairness, participants are continually comparing what is being offered and contemplated with their own sense of fairness. Regarding alternatives to agreement, what is addressed is the consequences of an impasse, that is, what are the choices in the absence of an agreement? The theory is that participants should not accept less than they can get elsewhere.

Finally, negotiation involves the exercise of personal and organizational power through the participants' decisions. More often than not, the result is agreement. Sometimes, however, the result is an impasse, in which case the mediator is expected to be resourceful and inspiring.

Process review

The primary assessment during the negotiation phase focuses on the reconciliation of the solutions generated during the option-generation phase in response to the needs listed in the education phase. The best agreements represent solutions that meet the participants' individual and shared needs to their maximum satisfaction.

"Now that we have a range of potential solutions, we need to review them and see how well they meet your mutual needs. What concerns do you have about these possible solutions?"

Often, after a diligent review, the participants conclude that their needs will be met by the solutions proposed. They consider the potential solutions to be sensible and, in the main, agreeable to both of them. With some minor fine-tuning and creative engagement, they usually reach agreement on a variety of issues and resolve their conflict. They then move to documenting their new understandings (the topic of the next chapter).

"From what I hear, you both seem comfortable with the solutions you identified during the brainstorming session. Obviously, we need to double check and make sure nothing is missing. However, this is great! You are almost done. Once we have clarity on exactly what it is you are agreeing to, I will document it in a format that you can sign."

When this does not happen easily, and especially when the issue has a zero-sum feel (if I win, you lose, and conversely, if you win, I lose), then it is wise to help the participants to assess their options by referring to acceptable standards of fairness, and also by considering the alternatives to agreement.

"While there are a number of ideas that you both like, I am aware that you disagree about the question of what to do with the performance rating. One of you wants it changed, while the other says it cannot be changed. I am wondering, is there any relevant policy document that informs you about how to deal with these situations?"

This helps the participants to be realistic about what is possible and to make revisions to their respective proposals. However, sometimes the ideal solution does not emerge naturally and the participants' proposals are relatively far apart.

When negotiations are competitive, and are seen as a choice between winning and losing, they are conducted by the exchange of initially extreme positions, which through a series of concessions normally leads to the midpoint between the first two reasonable offers presented. This is called the 'negotiation dance'.

Participants will try to anchor the negotiations at one or other end of the ballpark. People tend to give disproportionate weight to the first information they receive, especially in negotiations over money. This is called anchoring. Sometimes, people will make use of various tactics (such as anchoring) consciously, but often unconsciously. It is not your job to tell them how to negotiate. Be aware of the dynamics, monitor for surprise, and be ready to talk candidly in a joint session about this (and other tactics) as a shared dilemma. You could also coach in a private caucus about how to make an opening offer or a counter offer that is consistent with the participants' values and will help the collaborative momentum of the process.

The participants may be tempted to short-circuit the negotiation dance. There is a danger, however, that unless trust levels are high, an early midpoint settlement offer may be misinterpreted. This can happen due to one participant perceiving the other as an 'opponent', and devaluing the offer in reaction to this perception. You play a vital role (when the participants are in caucus) to facilitate the negotiation dance by being the 'neutral' conveyer of the settlement offers. You need to coach and support each participant until both are clear about what they are willing to offer.

Be wary of attempts to use competitive tactics that try to force agreement. They are usually aimed at securing an unfair advantage. There are a variety of these, including:

- starting with ridiculously high or low opening offers
- pretending an issue of little importance is significant so that it can be traded for disproportionate value later on
- asking for a small concession in respect of a new issue to close the deal at the end (referred to as 'nibbling', when someone keeps negotiating the deal even when it is supposedly done)
- threatening to take extreme action unless the other participant agrees.

Address these power-based moves, if necessary. Most generally, mediators tend to describe what they have noticed and invite confirmation. Although it is not always possible, this type of delicate intervention is best handled in the safety of a caucus.

Exploring fairness

"Expecting the world to treat you fairly because you are a good person is a little like expecting the bull not to attack you because you are a vegetarian."
Dennis Wholey

Through his study of the conflict-resolution behavior of primates, primatologist Frans de Waal has helped us to understand the deep roots of our human expectation to be treated fairly. He has concluded that we are inequity averse, which means we resent getting less yet feel uncomfortable when we get more.[1]

When participants disagree as to what is fair, your goal as mediator is to support them to find, and then apply, an acceptable standard of fairness. In general, mutually acceptable standards avoid an unproductive contest of wills. Often, the participants have distorted perceptions about what constitutes an acceptable range of fairness, and as a result they may make unrealistic demands. They read in the media about a large payment made to settle a discrimination case, and use that number as their reference to fairness.

"Trying to figure out what is fair in the circumstances is never easy. Either you do it, or you ask a judge (who does not know you) to decide, based on what both of you have said, and his or her interpretation of the law. I am wondering what sources of information you have access to that will give us all a sense of what your ballpark looks like. In other words, what is the range of 'possible', were you to put the matter to a judge?"

Until then, the participants can literally be in different universes, let alone ballparks. How do you go about getting them into the same ballpark so they can talk about fairness in a realistic manner? Independent standards that are acceptable to both participants can serve as reference points for fairness. The law has a lot to say about the conditions of employment. Another avenue to pursue could be employment contracts and the organizational policies and procedures of the company. These may give guidance as to what is expected.

Imagine a disagreement over how long it should take to complete a task. The manager thinks twenty minutes, while the employee thinks thirty. You really have no idea. However, you may ask if there are any credible benchmark studies that document how long, on average, the particular industry task should take. Or imagine a dispute between two employees in a restaurant kitchen. The one wants to store tomatoes in the refrigerator, while the other wants to store them on the shelf. You can only argue your case so many times before it gets old. So what do you do? You may invite the participants to look for guidance on the internet. *"Ask Google,"* you could say with a smile.

Help the participants to creatively explore other reference points together. Where do fresh produce outlets store their tomatoes? What about asking a chef? There is now legislation in California that requires cut tomatoes to be stored in a refrigerator. In a restaurant business, there may even be that level of specificity regarding how to store tomatoes.

Precedents and past practices color how we assess fairness, therefore court decisions and jury awards are very relevant when it comes to employment matters, as are benchmark comparisons with other similarly placed employees. These can be helpful when it comes to disputes over wages, but also to establish industry performance standards. These enquiries start to give us a sense of what others have done before in similar circumstances.

As much as we would like the law to be certain, so much depends on the circumstances. Often, the danger of asking what the law would say is that you end up paying attorneys to argue with one another! And yet, what happened to others in similar situations before plays a role in how we expect to be treated. Employees have an uncanny capacity to know these things, and to question whether they have been treated fairly.

My hope is that you are getting a feel for the task at hand. No matter the issue, there will be examples of what others have done before that can be used as a source of guidance as to what is fair.

That the standards agreed upon are acceptable to both participants is key. Other standards include, where appropriate, professional standards, moral standards and traditions. These can be particularly helpful in the context of relational disputes.

Sometimes, culture plays a role in determining what is acceptable in the circumstances. In our increasingly global economy, an interesting interface continues to emerge between national and organizational culture. It is not your role to impose your cultural values. Rather, facilitate the exploration of the specific standards that are possible, and allow the participants to find a standard that is credible to them both.

Helping participants to see that their demands are unrealistic is not easy, and certainly more difficult to accomplish in a joint session. It therefore often makes sense to explore perceptions of fairness and the consequences of not reaching an agreement in caucus.

Explore perceptions of standards through questions such as:
- "I wonder what others have done in similar situations?"
- "Is there a standard or reference point that would make sense to apply to your situation?"
- "What did you do last time?"
- "What does the contract/policy/regulation/law say?"
- "Is there a benchmark you could refer to?"
- "What is customary?"
- "Why don't you Google that?"

The alternatives analysis

"A bird in the hand is worth two in the bush."
English proverb

The alternatives analysis refers to the stage in the mediation where you ask the participants to look closely at what each will do if they do not reach an agreement. There is a real danger that this will be experienced as you, the mediator, applying pressure. It is for this reason that you need to be extremely tactful. It helps to explain the educational function of the alternatives analysis early on in the mediation.

Another difficulty is that stating the consequences of not agreeing can be interpreted as a threat. If this occurs, there is a real danger of an escalation in the conflict. Your job, therefore, is to manage the exchanges around the alternatives analysis so that no harm is done, which is why these conversations may also be best conducted in caucus.

Although it is not always made explicit, at some level both participants will be comparing what they can get at the negotiation table with what they believe they can get on their own, away from the table. And they will have views on how easy or difficult this will be to accomplish. If they consider the proposed offer to be too little, in other words, to represent 'crumbs', and they believe that there is a loaf of bread waiting for them away from the table, they may threaten to leave the table to get the full loaf. But is there, in fact, a loaf of bread? And if so, how will they get it? And what impact does the expressed intention to look for it have on the negotiation? These are the reality-testing questions that you need to ask the participants to help them to see the whole picture.

Imagine mediating an employment discrimination dispute where the employer makes an offer of $5,000 without an admission of wrong-doing. The employee takes offence, says the offer is insulting after what she has been through, that nothing less than $200,000 will do, and that she plans to go to court to get it, if necessary. Your task would be to gently help the participant to understand that there is no guarantee when one goes to court, that it takes a long time, costs a lot of money, and continues to be emotionally debilitating. Moreover, even if the relationship remains intact after the court case, the history of it will inevitably be a source of strain in the future.

"You sound confident that by going to court you will be awarded at least $200,000 as a result of what you went through. I do not mean to minimize your pain – you said it has been one of the most difficult periods of your life – but you have to ask yourself what guarantee you have that you will get that amount. Also, do you have a sense of what it will take, the risk notwithstanding, to get to court? What will it cost? How long will it take? Will there be any appeals? And what if it does not work out the way you expect?"

Participants give differing amounts of attention to what they will do if they are not able to work something out. Bear in mind that their expectations are often filtered through rose-tinted lenses so that they imagine the best possible outcome. Unless both of them have great self-awareness, these cognitive biases usually mean that both believe that they are more competent, honest, cooperative, and fair than the other. They may also rate their chances of success more highly than what is realistic. The fact that information tends to be filtered in a manner that leaves them feeling confident of being right often entraps participants, who continue to sink money into a failing course of action.

As I mentioned before, your role is to meet the participants where they are, and to be a trusty mountain guide. Helping them to shift their perspective from right and wrong to mutual responsibility for a shared challenge gives them a more realistic idea of what is possible. It is usually a powerfully liberating moment for the participants when this shift takes place.

Your ultimate role as mediator is to help both participants to reach an agreement. To do this, you need to carefully identify their alternatives to negotiation, both the good and the bad, and contrast them with the benefits of the potential solutions already on the table. Continue using the needs that were identified in the education phase as the ultimate yardstick. In other words, the quest remains the maximum satisfaction of the needs of both participants, whether through potential solutions they are contemplating together, or through the alternatives (the things they are considering to do on their own should they decide to leave the negotiating table).

No one goes to court to lose. Nor do people go over the heads of their bosses to be told that they are wrong. Helping participants to look at these unpleasant possibilities is one of the key levers that mediators use. By raising questions about potential outcomes that the participants may not like, you can often incline them towards working out a settlement agreement.

It takes considerable skill and tact to be able to use these levers in the service of the participants. In a real sense, the right to do so is earned through the rapport you build with each participant, especially during the joint sessions. Furthermore, any pressure you bring to bear arises from your asking how well the respective options are meeting, or the alternatives may meet, the participants' core needs. By gently acknowledging, validating, and then guiding, you should be able to ask the participants to take a careful and close look at what is real. And through direct yet friendly questions, you can review the full range of possible outcomes.

In the classic book, *Getting to YES*,[2] on which much of this approach to negotiation is based, the authors say that a negotiator ought to know both the best and the worst possible outcomes. Discussing the Best Alternative to a Negotiated Agreement (BATNA) is easy. Here you ask the participants to consider how it will be to win, with everything going right. But talking about the Worst Alternative to a Negotiated Agreement (WATNA) can be tough because you are asking them to consider how it will be to lose, with things not working out well. Often, the participants have not given the matter any thought and are shocked to realize what is at stake. If the worst alternative is too harsh for them to bear, reframe the conversation to the Most Likely Alternative to a Negotiated Agreement (MLATNA).

It is legitimate for you to sow the seeds of doubt. Do not feel guilty for doing so. Ask the overly confident participant whether there is any attorney who can guarantee a completely successful outcome. To the probable answer of "Not likely…" you can say: *"Then how sure are you of success?"* This line of reality-testing questioning usually works well with participants who are seeking something, whether it be job security or a payout. As noted earlier, participants usually like a sure thing when gains are at stake – generally, we like that bird in the hand. Your questions may sow seeds of doubt, but they will also create motivation to resolve the inner tension.

And for those participants – often managers or company representatives – for whom losses are at stake, their inclination (often unconscious) will be to take risks. For them, use an additional line of questions that focus on what is called the 'nuisance factor', which is an amount of money paid to make a distracting and costly situation go away. Bear in mind that doubt is doubt, and these participants may also recoil at the uncertainty, especially if you can hold up a clear image of what they have to gain by paying this money.

Organizations approach this issue differently. Some link the amount they are willing to pay to make the issue go away to that of their employment practices liabilities insurance deductible, which in the United States can be up to $50,000. Others offer a nominal amount, such as a few thousand dollars. Still others refuse to pay anything at all, as a matter of principle.

Your task, as mediator, is to make the participants aware of the risks of *not* paying this money, and to explore what is at stake. This may not feel right to you. It may smack of extortion. Furthermore, there is the danger of a precedent being set or a line being drawn. Yet you have to ask the participants to consider the business sense of paying the 'nuisance value'. Remember, you do not decide for them. Rather, you help them to see the extent to which the decision is being motivated by emotional, and perhaps irrational, reasons.

"This has to feel tough. It is not about fair. It is about who has the better alternative. And whether you like it or not, even if you are right, and you do win as you predict you will, it still may not make good business sense to ignore the possibility of making this go away now, without any admission of wrongdoing, for what is known as the 'nuisance value'."

Although it is impossible to make a non-emotional decision, there are options that appear to be so irrational and contrary to people's best interests that they warrant some consideration. Be very careful not to badger the participants, and once you see that they understand what you are asking them to consider, and are indeed considering these things, back off and remind them that it is their decision, not yours.

"At the end of the day, it is your decision. All I wanted to do was to make sure that you had considered the consequences of your choices. I can see that you have. I will respect what you decide."

Your goal is to make sure that each participant has looked realistically at the consequences of not agreeing, whether that includes the possibility of court, resignation, or termination of employment. These questions may help:

- *"What will you do if you do not reach an agreement?"*
- *"What alternatives do you have?"*
- *"What are the natural consequences of your choices if you do not agree?*

You need to be ever ready to remind the participants of their substantive, relational, identity and process needs (see Chapter 2, page 37, and Chapter 7, pages 89-91). You also need to remind them of the advantages and disadvantages of the various procedures available to address the conflict, and to make them aware of the hidden financial costs of a conflict for an organization, beyond the legal costs. Ask: *"Does it make sense not to settle, taking into consideration all the time that will be spent, the distraction and, of course, the risk?"*

As I have mentioned, helping the participants to review both the best and worst alternatives is a delicate process that should be approached with tact, and only after high levels of rapport have been established. Much of the time you will be able to help the participants to revise their decisions as they contemplate how the different alternatives may or may not meet their underlying needs.

At the end of the day, it is the participants who decide whether and on what terms to agree. What you need to do is to ensure that they decide only after having considered all the angles, including the unpleasant ones.

Reality-testing questions

In addition to supporting conversations that identify acceptable standards, and others that explore the consequences of not agreeing, it is also helpful to consider the questions of urgency, timeframes, costs, feasibility and desirability. These reality-testing questions help the participants to consider the viability of the proposed solutions.

They often lead to the restatement of needs, or the discovery of nuanced layers of needs. Ultimately, your role is to support realistic, attainable and sustainable agreements.

Reality-testing questions can be asked in joint session with both participants present. However, sometimes there is value in exploring the respective viability of solutions in private caucus.

Urgency

An issue may be urgent for one of the participants but not for the other, in other words, they both agree to the solution but not to the importance of making it happen soon.

"As I understand things, you would like to get revisions back within twenty-four hours. Can you both share a little about when the revisions need to be back, and why?"

It is not your role to decide. In supporting the participants to decide, you should help them to ensure that they agree about these types of details. Be alert to the ways these issues tend to surface residual tension, and how they sometimes bring out passive-aggressive behavior.

Timeframes

Focus the conversation on how much time is required to do what is contemplated. Again, there are often different perspectives about how long something will take. Getting the participants to talk about this allows them to reach realistic agreements.

"You both agree that it is worth doing. However, you disagree on how long it will take. Is there an independent reference point that will give us a better sense of how long it normally takes a person to do this?"

Costs

Some solutions are more costly than others. Getting a sense of the price range for a particular task or outcome can be helpful.

"Sounds like you both agree that costs are not an issue. You say you need the best possible equipment for this job. Is that correct?"

However, where a solution requires one participant to pay the other, for instance in the context of an employment discrimination allegation, the issue of how much will often be seen differently by the participants: the one paying will want to pay as little as possible; the one receiving payment will want as much as possible.

Feasibility and desirability

It can be helpful to ask the participants about the feasibility and desirability of their solution. Feasibility is more objective, while the desirability conversation will quickly surface any resistance to a solution. Sometimes a solution is possible, for instance a change to the performance review, but there is no willingness to change. It is better for resistance to be addressed as it surfaces than for it to come out later, possibly as resentment.

Power

Power, or influence, is necessary for the negotiation process to be effective. However, the chances of there being a perfect parity of power between the participants are remote. While it is true that extreme power imbalances may be a reason not to mediate (for example, where there has been physical violence), in general, mediators should be prepared to deal with imbalanced power dynamics. You will inevitably impact the power dynamics through your interventions. Through your mediation stance, you ought to be actively engaged in the promotion of collaboration.

One of the ways power is managed is through reference to acceptable standards, as discussed above. This is also sometimes referred to as a rights-based approach to dispute resolution, and is seen as a way of curtailing the raw exercise of power.

The other primary way you can manage power in a principled manner is through the reality-testing conversations you facilitate, and in particular the way you help the participants to conduct an alternatives analysis with a careful review of how their needs will best be met, whether through the options on the table or the alternatives away from the table.

Power ultimately comes down to how we influence others to do things our way. In a negotiation, one participant seeks an outcome that is apparently in conflict with what the other participant wants. Beyond our reframe from demands to needs, we should assess, and at times help, one or both of the participants to identify their own source of power. Both will have some degree of power, which is to a certain extent situational, for example, we walk out of a meeting with our boss where we are in a subordinate role into a meeting with our employees where we are in the more powerful position.

Power is a product of being in relationship and must be exercised to be effective. Power can be abused, as was starkly confirmed by the Stanford Prison experiment, where the 'student' guards were so abusive in the way they treated their 'student' prisoners that the experiment had to be aborted.[3] This is why reframing participants' demands and threats in the direction of needs, and conducting a thorough alternatives analysis, are so important.

Impasse-breaking techniques

"Resistance is a sign of an unmet need."
Kenneth Cloke

The mediator is not responsible for the settlement of any conflict or dispute. Your role is to assist the participants to make informed decisions. Only sometimes do they reach an agreement. Often, they do not. It is not your job to pressure the participants into a settlement.

Use your energy well by paying careful attention to where an impasse arises. Try not to waste your energy by getting frustrated when the participants are stuck. If this happens, they will look to you for guidance and inspiration. Rather than becoming defensive and taking their failure personally, I find it helpful to remind myself of what Kenneth Cloke has said (see quote above). With that in mind, I attend through empathic listening to discover what the source of the resistance may be.

Often, in the later stages of a mediation, the relational and identity needs may start to surface. If something has been forgotten or an issue has not been addressed, it is most likely that you will discover it.

Many mediators have 'laundry lists' of things they do to break an impasse. I prefer to say that you should keep mediating. Make sure of your postures and ultimate stance. Remain open and responsive to feedback. Be creative. Do something different. Think outside the box. Take risks. And always be that inspiring beacon of hope.

As mediators, we meet our participants on the road of life exactly where they are in terms of self-awareness and development, and we have to appreciate that they have good reasons for choosing not to agree. It is important to allow them *not* to work things out. For reasons that are often beyond our understanding, we have to respect that staying in conflict may be more important to them than working something out. The consequences are theirs to bear. We must be vigilant not to allow our hope for an outcome of settlement to get in the way of what the participants need.

'Laundry list'

For those of you who want such a list of things to try in order to break an impasse, this has been my favorite one for years. It is adapted from the Veteran's Affairs website.[4]

1. Take a break. Often, things have a way of looking different when you return.
2. Ask the participants if they agree to set the issue aside temporarily and go on to something else – preferably an easier issue.
3. Ask the participants to explain their perspectives on why they appear to be experiencing an impasse. Sometimes, they need to focus consciously on their deadlock.
4. Ask the participants: *"What would you like to do next?"* Then pause expectantly. Or, say: *"Frankly, it looks like we are really stuck on this issue. What do you think we should do?"* These questions help them to actively share the burden of the impasse.
5. Ask each participant to describe his/her fears (but do not appear condescending, and do not make them feel defensive).
6. Try a global summary of both participants' perspectives and what they have said so far, 'telescoping' the issue so that they can see where they are stuck in the context of the bigger picture. Sometimes, the impasse issue will then seem less important.

7. Restate all the things they have agreed about so far, praise them for their work and accomplishments, and validate that they have come a long way. Then, ask something like: *"Do you want to let all that get away from you?"*

8. Ask the participants to focus on the ideal future. For example, ask each of them: *"Where would you like to be [concerning the matter about which they are experiencing an impasse] a year from now?"* Follow the answers with questions about how they might get there.

9. Suggest a trial period or plan. For instance: *"Sometimes people will agree to try an approach for six months and then meet again to discuss how it is working."*

10. Help the participants to define what they need by developing criteria for an acceptable outcome. Say: *"Before we focus on the outcome itself, would you like to try to define the qualities that any good outcome should have?"*

11. Be a catalyst. Offer a 'what if' that is only marginally realistic or even a little wild, just to see if their reactions result in them becoming unstuck.

12. With permission, float a possible solution. Say: *"Sometimes, we see participants to this kind of dispute agree to something like the following…"*

13. Try role-reversal. Say: *"If you were Harry, why do you think your proposal would not be workable?"* Or: *"If you were Sally, why would you accept your proposal?"*

14. Another role-reversal technique is to ask each participant to briefly assume the other's role and then to react to the impasse issue. You can also ask each of them to play devil's advocate and argue against his or her own position.

15. Ask the participants if they would like to try an exercise to ensure that they understand each other's position before mediation ends. Ask Harry to state his position and give his reasons. Ask Sally to repeat what she heard. Then ask Harry if Sally's repetition is accurate. Repeat this procedure for Sally. Listen and look for opportunities to clarify.

16. Ask: *"What would you be willing to offer if Harry agreed to accept your proposal?"*

17. Use reality-testing questions to examine the participants' BATNAs, WATNAs and MLANTAs more deeply. For example, ask: *"What do you think will happen if this goes to court?"* Draw out the emotional, financial and other costs of litigation and delay.

18. If all else fails, suggest (or threaten) ending the mediation. Due to their investment in the process, participants often will not want it to fail, and may suddenly be able to move forward. This approach is useful where one participant may be hanging on because s/he enjoys the attention the process provides, or enjoys the other participant's discomfort.

---

[1] http://www.mediate.com/articles/what.cfm
[2] Fisher et al., 1991.
[3] http://www.prisonexp.org
[4] http://www.va.gov/ADR/Impasse.asp

Chapter 10
The Closing Phase

*"The most successful agreements are
balanced, behaviorally specific, and written."*
Daniel Dana

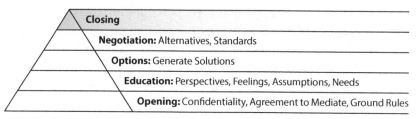

The Mediation Process

The hard work of the preceding phases of the mediation prepares the participants for the final phase of the process, during which the mediator formalizes the agreement in a manner acceptable to the participants and designs an implementation and monitoring procedure.[1]

A settlement agreement is an oral or written contract in which the terms and conditions of a resolved conflict are evidenced by mutually acceptable promises. Closure is not only achieved by signing the agreement but also through the degree of emotional completeness that the participants experience. The conflict is over! It may not be what was expected. It may not be ideal in every respect. But there is a feeling of satisfaction that comes from knowing one has showed up and worked hard to resolve a conflict in the most creative way possible.

In truth, there will probably be a mixture of feelings. As mediator, be ready to acknowledge disappointment and frustration if the process did not end as one or both of the participants had hoped it would. Also empathize with any relief, satisfaction and pride at what has been accomplished.

For a conflict to be successfully resolved at a behavioral level, all the underlying needs of the participants must be addressed in a manner perceived by both of them to be satisfactory. These needs are not only transactional and substantive; relational and identity needs are also important, especially in the workplace. When we focus on the tangible issues, we often overlook the importance of these more emotional aspects. It is sensible to support the participants to make explicit their agreements about how they are going to support the relationship and one another. When floating ideas, remember that your role is to *not* decide.

The mediator is usually not responsible for the process that brought the participants to the mediation. You are, however, responsible for the mediation process itself. Hopefully, both participants will have observed you doing your best to be balanced, tactful, resourceful and inspiring. Your mediation stance should leave them feeling good about the experience.

Ideally, everyone who needs to authorize the agreement should be present at the mediation. If any such persons are absent, their written consent should be obtained. Once you are satisfied that due authorization has been obtained, the terms and conditions of the agreement should be summarized in the presence of the participants. If the agreement is to be documented in writing and signed, draft the terms and let the participants review the draft. Once they are satisfied with it, finalize the agreement and prepare for the signing ceremony.

The moment of agreement is the point at which the participants sign. Usually, they will then shake hands or cement the agreement in a similar way. Look for ways to support the closure and to strengthen their level of commitment to the agreement. As you do this, be careful to maintain the mediation stance so that you are ready to meet the challenge in case misunderstandings, questions, resistance or new issues arise. Do not rush things – mediation is not about pressuring participants to sign at the eleventh hour.

Reaching agreement is often difficult and usually there are disappointments and/or regrets. However, the participants should not feel that they are under duress, and their right to self-determination should reign supreme.

Sometimes, there is no resolution of the conflict. As mediator, you still need to attend to the closure of the process. Acknowledge the participants' contributions. Keep the door to collaboration open and encourage them as they move forward. You should also honor their courage to have disagreed, and to have done what felt right for them.

Documenting agreements

"Recording deals in mutually acceptable terms will help protect against selective memory loss in the future."
Daniel Dana

Sometimes, the participants will prefer to shake hands and commit orally to the terms of the agreement. However, given the frailty of human memory, it makes sense to collate into a document your careful summaries of the issues on which the participants have agreed. This minimizes the possibility of disagreements in the future over what they had agreed upon. Depending on the circumstances, it may be sufficient to simply confirm the understandings in an e-mail.

When you draft the final agreement document, the challenge is to be clear about the intent. Specify (without trying to micromanage) who does what, and when and how things should be done. Ideally, the agreement should be balanced, and both participants should have committed to doing things for each other.

The agreement should provide objective criteria that can be used to monitor whether it is being implemented as agreed. A useful test to determine whether the monitoring criteria are clear is to ask whether others who were not at the mediation would know if the agreement has been adhered to or not.

The reality is that no matter how much time the participants have spent reaching clarity on the nature and extent of their commitments, the future has an irreducible element of uncertainty. Despite their best efforts, they cannot anticipate and foresee everything that may happen. The agreement therefore needs to be flexible enough to meet the participants' emerging reality, and should allow them to adjust and fine-tune, as needed.

It is worth remembering that formal agreements are normally referenced when the relationship is no longer functional. As long as the participants are talking and are in a relationship, they will find ways to work things out. Despite a clear agreement, breakdowns do occur and should not be cause for alarm. A future dispute-resolution clause goes a long way to ensuring that any challenges that do arise are treated as opportunities for creativity. It helps to normalize the reality that there will most likely be challenges in the future.

Appendix 5 on page 167 is a sample settlement agreement that includes clauses which show typical relational disputes. I encourage you to consider them when drafting any agreement. Once you have prepared a draft, make it available for both participants to review. If you have a computer with a projector, consider using that as a way of focusing their attention on the text at the same time.

At this point, it may seem more convenient to conduct the final negotiation over the wording of the agreement by e-mail. Be aware that this blessing can also be a curse if not managed with care. Unless you are in caucus, be sure to include both participants in all your e-mails. More often than not, the inconvenience of a face-to-face meeting is worth it when you factor in the potential consequences of an e-mail flare-up or fallout.

What an agreement should address

Why

This is the vision and intent which informs the agreement. It is often accomplished in a context-setting recital.

"Harry and Sally have taken the time to reach new understandings about the 2013 performance review. This agreement addresses the issue and documents how it will be implemented."

Who

The people responsible for the agreement are normally named next. Their signatures also appear at the end of the agreement. This can be stated simply.

"The Parties to this Settlement Agreement are Harry and Sally."

It is also important to be clear about who is responsible for carrying out the terms of the agreement. Be careful not to make commitments for those who are not at the table, or to make aspects of the agreement conditional on such people's support.

"This Agreement is subject to the review and approval of the Director of Operations."

What

This refers to the conditions under which the substantive content of the agreement will be fulfilled.

"Harry agrees to recommend to the Director of Operations to formally change the end-of-year performance rating of Sally from a 2 to a 4 with respect to the Communication and Team Work standard. This agreement is conditional on the performance rating being changed as contemplated."

And:

"Sally agrees to withdraw, with prejudice, her claim that she was discriminated against on the basis of her gender and age when given an annual performance rating of 2 in respect of the Communication and Team Work standard in 2013."

When

This is the explicit timeframe which sets out when performance should commence and for how long the agreement will endure.

"This change will be made within two weeks of the Operation Director's approval. It will be effective from the date of the original performance review."

Where

This aspect of the agreement refers to the exact place or location where performance will be carried out.

"The change will be reflected in Sally's formal personnel file held by HR in the company's head office in San Francisco, CA."

What if...

These are the steps to follow should there be a conflict or dispute. In the case of a relational dispute they can be more informal.

"We agree that if we have concerns, suggestions or questions about an issue related to one another, we will talk privately together and in confidence. If we cannot reach an agreement on an issue on our own, we will look to HR for support and guidance, preferably through another mediation session."

In the case of an employment discrimination complaint they can be more formal.

"If Sally believes that the Company has not complied with any of the terms and/or conditions of this Agreement, Sally shall notify, in writing, the Director of Human Resources, informing him/her of the alleged noncompliance within 30 days of when Sally knew or should have known of the alleged noncompliance. Sally may request that the terms of this Agreement be specifically implemented or, alternatively, that the complaint be reinstated for further processing from the point that processing ceased."

The signing ceremony

To the extent that the psychological goal of this phase is closure and a sense of completion, it helps to make use of commitment rituals that increase the levels of accountability.

The agreement is a real accomplishment. When you get to the top of the mountain, you smile, look around, and are moved both by the beauty of what you see and the magnitude of the accomplishment. The participants in your mediations should experience something similar.

Most of the time, it will be you and the two participants. However, where you are mediating on behalf of a manager, it often makes sense to include that person, especially if the participants have agreed to share a copy of the settlement agreement with him or her. In this event, consider including the manager at the signing of the Agreement to Mediate, and include a clause that states that the Settlement Agreement will be shared with the manager.

"The confidentiality of the mediation process will be respected. We are comfortable sharing this agreement with our manager and anyone else with a legitimate need to know its contents."

This is a wonderful opportunity to praise and congratulate the participants on their accomplishments. The manager can do the same, and express appreciation that the participants made use of the opportunity to mediate. Apart from ritualizing the signing ceremony, consider the role of the handshake as a powerful way of signaling agreement. Another good idea is to have a meal together.

Mediator feedback

As mediator, being open to feedback is part of your stance. It may be appropriate to solicit informal feedback from both participants as to how the mediation went. As more and more organizations move away from the use of mediation on an *ad hoc* basis, expect to increasingly see the use of written mediation evaluations at the end of mediations. I have included a sample evaluation as Appendix 6 on page 171.

---

[1]   Moore, 2003.

Chapter 11
The Structured Caucus

"The separate meetings are a venue for significant developments in the mediation as a whole, not an optional adjunct to the process, to be used only when things get sticky."

John Winslade and Gerald Monk

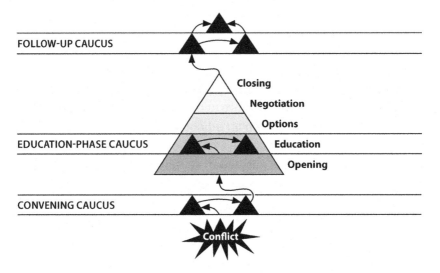

This chapter provides further information about the more structured use of the caucus as part of the convening, education and follow-up stages. Each is addressed in turn.

The convening caucus

"The pre-caucus affords each party the opportunity to be heard and understood."
Gregorio Billikopf

The caucus that the mediator conducts with each of the participants to convene a mediation is a best practice, although not an essential element of the mediation process (as is suggested by the quote that opens this chapter). These meetings are especially useful in the context of ongoing relational conflicts.

The primary purpose of the convening caucus is to prepare and equip both of the participants for success in the actual mediation. Participants are given a full and unfettered opportunity to express their perspectives of the situation. They are given this opportunity again during the education phase, but in the convening caucus they are alone with you, so there is no concern about the impact of their statements on the other participant.

During each convening caucus, attend to the participant with whom you are working through your mediation stance, paying particular attention to your empathic listening skills. You want to ensure that each person has been 'heard and understood' in the fullest sense. The participant should do most of the talking. You may start the conversation with something along these lines:

"Thanks for agreeing to meet today. This is an opportunity for you to express your perspective on the situation at hand. Tell me what happened in the way that makes sense to you."

As the participant's perspective is shared, ask clarifying questions. Remember, however, that this is *not* a fact-finding interview, and that your questions may throw the person off track. You may also summarize what is being said, and make sure to do a global summary towards the end.

First listen to and understand the participant's perspective, then attend to the other tasks associated with the convening caucus, which are to explain the mediation process, to provide any necessary coaching, and to gain the participant's commitment to participate in the mediation. An additional goal of the meeting is to take the 'emotional pulse', and to gather information to help you understand the conflict dynamics at play, which may be complex.

Your explanation of the process should be brief. It often works to explore mediation through a question-and-answer session. The participants should feel safe talking about the conflict and understand that:

- your role is to *not* decide
- you will strive to be balanced in all you do
- the process is voluntary
- both the convening caucus and the mediation itself will be confidential.

As you listen you will gain an impression of each participant's emotions, as well as their maturity and self-awareness. For instance, some people may be familiar with good communication practices. Others may be emotionally intelligent and competent at conflict resolution, whether it be through direct negotiation or a forgiveness process. Most people will have some but not all of these attributes. Remember to meet your participants where they are on the path of life.

During the convening caucus, do your best to prepare the participants for the mediation. Encourage them to consider the role of communication, negotiation and forgiveness, and support their skill development. For example:

"As I listened, it sounded like you are unhappy about your most recent performance review, and also some other things, like the way you communicate in public and in front of your peers. I got the impression that you have been embarrassed at times? I would like to share a communication technique that may be helpful. Maybe you already know it. It is called an 'I' statement. Here is how it works. As part of your preparation for the joint mediation session, I invite you to write down as many 'I' statements as you can, for all the things that have some emotional charge and that you need to communicate."

In addition to coaching on the use of the 'I' statement, it also helps to point out the limitations of memory, and the way we tend to make assumptions about one another's motives. These somewhat philosophical conversations should be conducted with great care so as not to undo the good work of just listening. However, it is often easier to plant these seeds in the convening caucus than it is later on in the process.

It is a good idea to take notes of the items covered in the meeting with the one participant in order to cover similar ground with the other. After the convening caucus, you should have a good sense of each participant's motivation and of why the mediation is taking place. Ideally, you want to gain their commitment to participate in the mediation with a full understanding of what that entails. Your earlier explanation of the mediation process allows you to ask something like this:

"As we wrap up this session, I need to make sure that you want to participate in the mediation. Now is a good time to ask any residual questions. If you do not have any, can I assume that you will participate?"

Your final goal, to take the 'emotional pulse' of the conflict, is something that you do on your own. This involves identifying the issues, and getting a sense of whether they are mainly transactional or relational.

The convening caucus should help you to determine the participants' capacity to talk about their emotions, in the present, about the past. You will also probably get a sense of whether each participant hails from an avoidant, volatile or collaborative family, and whether destructive behaviors are at play. Also, you will probably understand the assumptions each participant is making about the other. This can be helpful, especially as you will receive information from the one that the other does not have.

Education-phase caucus

The main difference between the convening caucus and the education-phase caucus is the stage at which each is held. The convening caucus is conducted before the first joint session, while the education-phase caucus is conducted immediately after the opening statement.

The purpose of the two caucuses is the same, save that the participants have agreed to mediate, so it is unlikely that there will be concerns about commitment or the mediation process itself.

The focus of the education-phase caucus is to give both participants the freedom to express themselves fully. Coach as necessary, provide motivation, and take the emotional pulse. All of this will be helpful when you reconvene the joint mediation session. When you do, you should allow each of the participants to share their perspective in the joint session as they would if you had not held a caucus with each of them separately.

Follow-up

"A mediator can make use of what social psychologists call the 'audience effect' in following up with participants at some agreed time in the future."
Daniel Dana

One of the reasons coaching works well is that the person being coached 'contracts out' to the coach the responsibility for accountability regarding the goals. The coach can then follow up regularly with the person s/he has coached to see how things are going, without having to take responsibility for the accomplishment of the goals.

When mediators follow up after a mediation that has produced an agreement, they are essentially doing the same thing. You do not take responsibility for the implementation of the agreement, but you do create a forum for the participants to report back on how things are going, and to explain both the successes and the challenges they have experienced since reaching the agreement.

Also, mediators do benefit from the 'audience effect' that managerial mediation pioneer Daniel Dana points to in the preceding quote. This effect refers to the fact that participants tend to be more motivated to keep their agreements when they have the 'audience' of the mediator, in a similar way that they tend to devalue offers made by each other, but not those made by the mediator.

There was a time when I considered the follow-up meetings to be a courtesy – something non-essential but good to do. I am increasingly of the view that these meetings are a vital part of any mediation, especially in workplace mediations where the participants have worked out new behavioral arrangements.

Reasons to follow up

First and foremost, follow-up meetings signal that you care. The participants know that you share in their desire to succeed. In addition, they signal your realism. We all know how hard it is to change habits. Over time, people develop dysfunctional ways of relating to one another. Agreeing to change behavior is one thing; actually changing it is another.

Furthermore, follow-up meetings create an opportunity to fine-tune or make adjustments to the agreement, based on life experience. Doing this is not a sign of failure but of maturity. By following up, you are creating an opportunity for the participants to troubleshoot and consolidate lessons learnt. The entire focus of the follow-up meeting is learning. Following up should not be about blame but about continuous improvement.

How to follow up

My preference is to follow up about 45 days after a mediation has produced a behaviorally specific agreement. It is often a good idea to start with a caucus with each of the participants. You can caucus face-to-face; however, it may be convenient at times to check in with each of the participants by way of a phone call. It is a good idea to follow the individual caucuses with a joint session.

Whether in caucus or in a joint session, establish rapport by listening reflectively to whatever is said. Validate the emotions at play, and explore whether it is possible to reframe any frustration as care, disappointment as commitment, or anxiety as courage.

Once you sense that the participants are comfortable and ready to open up, orient them to what you are about to do. Remind them that the process is still confidential. You can use open-ended questions, such as:

- *"What aspects of the agreement you reached have been working well?"*
- *"What have you done differently since reaching the agreement?"*
- *"What has the other participant done differently since reaching the agreement?"*
- *"What aspects of the agreement are causing frustration/disappointment/anxiety?"*

If necessary, you may also use close-ended questions, such as:

- *"Have you been following the terms of your new agreement?"*
- *"Have you been meeting regularly as proposed?"*
- *"When last did you look at the agreement?"*

When you follow up in a joint meeting, get the participants to share specific situations that have been challenging and that illustrate the dynamics between them. Based on what they share, you may do some additional skills building. You can then do what I call a 'Take Two' – you ask them to replay the situation and, with some supportive coaching and encouragement, help them to see how it could have worked out differently.

Remember that in many ways mediators are coaches, asking the accountability questions while leaving the responsibility for making and implementing decisions where it belongs – with the participants themselves.

Chapter 12

Harry and Sally

"What I hear, I forget,
What I see, I remember,
What I do, I understand."
Confucius

When I train HR Managers mediation skills in person, I first explain the theory. I then demonstrate the skill and allow them to practice. Thereafter, we review our learning, based on the different experiences the students have had practicing the new skill. We follow this format as we move through the various stages of the mediation process. My explanation of the theory behind the skill and the accompanying knowledge is what I have articulated in the preceding chapters of this book.

Now you need to practice mediation yourself. Typically, this need is addressed through role-plays during face-to-face training. Ultimately, however, it will be the mediations that you convene and facilitate that will be your best practice ground, so try to look for opportunities to convene mediations. You will also get practice by adopting the mediation stance more and more in your work life.

The practice of mediating allows you to learn from your experience. You will do things knowing why, and you will do things wondering why. As you go along, you will get feedback – information about how things are going. Your adoption of the mediation stance, and your sensitive interventions in the spirit of collaboration, will help you to develop implicit and intuitive knowledge about what is effective and what is not.

Usually, I demonstrate mediation skills by asking two students to play the role of participants. This chapter is intended to address that need for demonstration. Most basically, it is a narrative description of an imaginary conflict between two fictitious participants, Harry and Sally. While you read, try to imagine how an actual conflict could be resolved through mediation.

Background

Harry and Sally have worked together for ten years. Since the initial 'honeymoon' phase that followed Harry's decision to hire Sally, they have had a bumpy ride. The work is always done, but the two of them have yet to establish a comfortable working relationship. Problems always seem to arise. They have managed to keep their issues private, but one can sense that there is always something unpleasant beneath the surface.

Early on in their relationship, Sally discovered that Harry was direct in his manner and had a short fuse. Harry observed how Sally was quiet and somewhat indirect. Of course, at that point of formation, both were making an effort and giving one another the benefit of the doubt. When that stopped, and the first signs of conflict emerged, both ran for cover after any 'eruptions'.

As a result, Harry and Sally became less open and more guarded with each other. One could say they became less real and more interested in what it would take to avoid the conflict. After all, they were professionals. For brief moments, they would establish and follow productive communication and conflict-resolution paths, but for the most part, things were unsettled and tense.

Convening the mediation

A couple of days ago, things came to a head. The annual performance results were announced and, to her shock, Sally saw that she had been given a 2 for Communication and Teamwork. In the past, she had received a couple of 5s and 3s, but mainly 4s, for this category. But never a 2! Stunned, she called her colleague and friend, Jane, for advice.

Having taken one of the conflict-resolution skills training courses that the company offered, Jane did a good job of listening to Sally. She let her express both her disbelief and indignant anger at what had happened. What was clear was that it was unacceptable to Sally and she was going to do what it took to get it changed, even if it meant having to say that Harry was being discriminatory. Sally expressed the opinion that there was no way Harry would have done this to football-loving Chuck, another of his subordinates.

As she fumed, Sally related how Harry had actually had the gall to snub her in a team meeting the previous week. He had abruptly ended a meeting before Sally had had a chance to make her contribution. It was embarrassing. Talking of embarrassment, Sally now reviewed some of the more outrageous beratings she had had to endure. Like the time Harry had asked her why she tried so hard! Or the 'you are not such an angel' routine. Not any more, she said. This had to stop.

After Sally had put down the phone, she immediately walked over to HR, where the receptionist correctly identified her as an 'angry' employee. According to the procedures in place regarding this situation, Sally was immediately given access to any available manager. You!

As you leave your office to meet with Sally for the first time, remind yourself of rule number one. Adopt the mediation stance. Breathe deeply and allow your busy world to drop away as you focus your attention on your meeting with this employee in need of support.

Shake hands as you greet Sally. Your tone should be soft and soothing. Immediately tune into Sally's emotional state – seething outrage.

Quickly guide Sally to the conference room, shut the door, pour two glasses of water and sit down. Do not rush. Instead, be steady and deliberate as you attend to the emerging situation. As you sit down, ask Sally with interest and care: "*What happened?*"

This is exactly what Sally wants to hear. She needs to be able to tell someone what has happened. She also needs acknowledgement of the emotional discomfort she is in. Of course, she would want whatever was wrong corrected. Why would she not?

Everything in your demeanor tells Sally that you want to understand her. As she drinks the water and relaxes in the pleasant conference room, she is soothed.

Then Sally tells you what has happened – a similar version of the discussion she has had with Jane. Your calm attitude and your genuine interest and care, as well as your good communication skills, especially as an empathic listener, help Sally to calm down more.

You agree that the situation needs attention. You empathize with the fact that, as it stands, things are troubling for Sally. Clearly, this is upsetting. You explain your role as the HR Manager. You tell her that you can set up a facilitated meeting, called a mediation, at which Harry would also be present, to give them both an opportunity to resolve the conflict.

You say that you will meet with her again after you have spoken to Harry. At this point, you make no effort to explore the substantive, relational or identity conflict with Sally, other than to suggest mediation as an appropriate way forward. You maintain the mediation stance.

You take the time to explain why you think mediation would be a good idea in the circumstances. At first, Sally may be hesitant. She may feel that nothing will ever change, and that Harry should be taken to task, and the rating on the performance review changed forthwith. You allow her to express her feelings of frustration, disappointment and fear.

Sally is now much more relaxed and composed. She is still energized, however, and ready to take on the challenge. She also knows that she will have to channel her energy, but that at least something is being done. You, the mediator, have been respectful and considerate, and have listened without challenge. The only pressure has been to meet with Harry in mediation. However, deep down Sally knows that what they need to do is talk. You tell her that you will get back to her shortly.

Now you call Harry. You have worked together in the past and have a good understanding. *"I just saw Sally,"* you say, and before you can continue, Harry sighs, replying: "Let me guess. It is her performance review. Well, it is not going to change, unless it is over my dead body!"

"Ok! Sounds like we have something going on. What is your perspective?" you ask, respectfully.

"Well, she got the 2 for not rescheduling the one-on-one meeting we are meant to have every second week," Harry responds, with mounting anger. "Although that is hardly the end of the world and should not impact her pay, I am just tired of her excuses. The last time I told her that if she messed up again, she would pay!"

You: *"That sounds frustrating! I do not want to interfere in things or make matters worse. But I believe I can help. Some of us in HR have been trained to be mediators. We are making ourselves availa-*

ble to mediate short meetings to explore solutions early, before things get worse. Would you be willing to come to a meeting with Sally? I would be the mediator. It would be good to clear the air and get both of you back on track. You do not have to agree to anything, only to participate."

At this point, you do not know much, besides that there is a conflict emerging that centers on a performance review. Based on Harry's words "over my dead body", you know that it is effectively a dispute. Sally held back in her conversation with you about Harry being discriminatory.

Harry and Sally have an ongoing relationship and the work they do is important. Helping them to resolve their issues and get on with one another is crucial; otherwise they will just keep finding new issues to fight over. You have seen that they do not see eye to eye and both have strong feelings, so any resolution will need to address their emotions. Until now, open conflict has been avoided. Their problems with each other have mainly been experienced as a dangerous and unsettling undercurrent.

Through your nimble adoption of the mediation stance, you have very quickly helped convene a mediation. Both Harry and Sally have started to trust you. You have inspired their confidence by the clear way you have talked about the mediation process and its benefits. It helps that the mediation is being set up when things are fresh and in need of resolution.

Process choices

Based on your assessment of the situation, you decide that a convening caucus would be ideal. While you have the authority to conduct informal mediations such as this one without the approval of your Line Manager and HR Director, you need their consent to take the extra time to conduct the convening caucus with each participant. One of the useful side benefits of this policy is that it empowers HR managers to take care of the run-of-the-mill situations, and effectively flag those that are more challenging.

Beth is your HR Director. She has worked in employee relations. She transitioned from being the head of Organizational Development into her current leadership role. She has faced her own conflict demons and is a champion for the recognition of conflict management as a core competency which is directly linked to performance reviews. She has participated in many employment discrimination mediation cases with attorneys.

Beth gets it. She knows that mediation works for more formal cases with external mediators. She believes there is no reason for it not to work internally as well. She agrees it would be a good idea to involve Bill, Harry's boss, but not before checking with Harry. Bill should attend the first meeting and help set the tone. Beth believes in being thorough. Not rushing. Taking one step at a time. Without being consciously aware of it, she also adopts the mediation stance.

Bill and Beth have a good working relationship and Beth believes that he will not want to be burdened with the details of the conflict. Bill knows them both as quality employees who form a vital backbone in his department. Beth expects that Bill will agree to come to the first meeting and will want to support them to work something out.

The convening caucus

Sally

You meet with Sally first. You have an hour together. You welcome her and quickly put her at ease as you guide the conversation. This time, instead of asking what happened, you say to her: *"Please share your perspective on how it is that we are having this conversation today. How do you make sense of it? How do you feel about it? And what do you need to move forward?"*

Sally: "That is a good question. How did I get here? Sometimes I wonder about that too. Basically, most recently…" Sally then recounts what she had previously told you about the unfairness of the performance review, and also about the meeting where she was snubbed. But this time, she adds more. She talks about incidents where Harry would lose his cool, have a meltdown, and say and do hurtful and embarrassing things. She tells you that afterwards he would apologize.

"He likes to be left alone, although in the beginning he said that I should always feel free to see him. And he had kept true to his word.

Another thing that happened that is consistent with the way he publically humiliates me is that he snubbed me at a recent team meeting. That was way out of line. At the very least, he owed me an explanation and apology for why he so abruptly ended the meeting, just before it was my turn to give my report. I was humiliated and felt angry. It is so unfair. Sometimes I wonder why we cannot get along."

You: *"How would you like to get along?"*

Sally: "Honestly, I don't know. I have given up. When I started, I thought he was great. He seemed to want to include me, and gave me access to him. He generally likes to be left alone. Anyway, I was wondering, what are my rights about the performance review? If we do not work something out, what will happen then?"

You: *"Well, if you do not agree in mediation about how to resolve the issue, you will be able to appeal the performance review to your Director, Bill. He will look into it and make a decision."*

Sally: "He will just side with Harry. What I want is to be treated with respect, and not to have to hear him say he is sorry for his temper tantrums. I know he is working on it. And actually it has improved, but my performance review is not fair."

You: *"Mediation offers a great opportunity for you in these circumstances. You want to address your dissatisfaction with the performance review. You do not trust Bill to be impartial. You also want to get to the bottom of things so that you can improve your relationship with Harry. Whatever is going on, you would like to clear the air and move forward."*

Sally: "That's it! That is so important. We have to improve our relationship. It is ridiculous that we just cannot get along!"

You: *"Do you have any further questions about the mediation? I am feeling optimistic. My sense is that you are ready to get real with Harry and sort things out. Who knows, you may be surprised. Giving more thought to what you want to say is a good idea. Spend more time thinking about what you need. Also think about how you have been feeling and how you would like to feel in future. I will be there and will do my best to keep the conversation productive and focused."*

Sally: "I think I am clear about the mediation. We will both be able to say what happened, and you will be there to help us work something out, but you will not decide, like a judge would."

You may also tell Sally about the likelihood of Bill's involvement as Harry's boss, and coach her on the use of 'I' statements (see pages 49-51), for instance in each of these situations: the performance review, the meeting where she felt she was cut off, and the occasions when she was embarrassed by a comment that Harry made in public.

Harry

Next, you make an appointment to meet with Harry in his office. He is ready for you and has clearly given the matter some thought.

Harry: "You know, the way I see it, I had to take a stand. It has been going on for so long now that it is ridiculous. Sally can be so frustrating."

You: *"Keep going. This has clearly been a source of irritation. I can see you get angry just thinking about it. What can you do about it?"*

Harry: "Well, I have a good mind to involve Bill. I have shielded Sally for too long. I have never taken our problems to Bill. I am more private, but I think he needs to be involved now."

You: *"I agree that involving Bill is a good idea because it allows him to encourage both of you to work something out, without taking sides. He will only come to the first meeting, when we sign the Agreement to Mediate."*

Harry: "I don't really know. I feel I have tried everything. It really was not that bad in the beginning. And technically she is sound, actually great. So we get the work done. But we seem to rub each other up the wrong way."

Harry pauses before proceeding.

"I know I have to watch my anger. I am working on that. Most of the time, I am in control. And I am getting better. But there has to be more to it. You know, I hope we can get to the bottom of this because we need Sally, and she would be hard to replace."

"Mostly, we have to sort out the one-on-one meetings. She has to show me some respect because I am her manager. I want her to show up and take responsibility for those meetings. If I do not see her giving, I feel that I cannot give either. I don't have more time now, but I am prepared to give mediation a chance."

You: *"Harry, I know you are busy. I appreciate your willingness to participate. It sounds like you would like to work something out about Sally's recent performance review, the situation with meetings, and generally how you are going to work together in future. This is an opportunity for both of you. I am hopeful!"*

Room set-up

You choose not to use either of the conference rooms in the HR department, preferring the private and out-of-the-way rooftop recreation area. Although this area is usually used for special functions, it has a conference room at the back of the lounge. The room has comfortable chairs with arm rests and faces the rooftop garden.

On the day of the first meeting, you have positioned the chairs carefully. You will sit on one side, with your back to the window. Harry and Sally will sit next to each other, facing the garden. Bill will sit at the head of the table, closest to the door. You have placed a jug of water and glasses on the table, as well as a bowl of peanuts and raisins. You have put up a *Meeting in Progress* sign on the door.

Time and duration

You have booked the room for a time that suits Harry, Sally and Bill, and have notified them of the exact location in an e-mail. Attached to the e-mail is the Agreement to Mediate document.

The opening statement

Here is an example of an opening statement for the meeting. Do not copy this statement exactly but draft an opening statement that resonates with you and is reflective of your own voice.

"I am encouraged that you have both chosen to mediate. It tells me that you both want to work something out. I am also happy that Bill could make it. He will say a couple of words before he leaves."

Bill: "Thanks. Yes, I just wanted to say that I value you both and know you are in good hands. I was a little surprised but understand that you have some issues to work out. Please make the best of this opportunity."

You continue.

"It appears that, although you are in conflict, you are both open to working something out. I am encouraged. And in all honesty, I am unaware of any reason for your not being able to work it out.

"We are here today to focus on your working relationship and to see what agreements you can reach to help it thrive.

"After I have completed my opening statement, each of you will have an uninterrupted opportunity to share your perspectives of the situation. I encourage you both to identify your needs and talk about how you feel and what you think. After each of you has had a turn, and we have had a full opportunity to explore the situation, we will work together to develop solutions. I may make suggestions based on what I have seen others do in similar situations, but as I will clarify in more detail later, I will always fall short of telling you what to do.

"After I have finished the opening statement and we have signed the Agreement to Mediate, I will ask Sally to share her perspective first. We have to start with someone, and the norm is to start with the person who contacted us in HR to request mediation. This is not set in stone, and if it makes more sense for Harry to go first, we can talk about it.

"My role is to support you to reach your own agreements. To that extent, you are responsible for any resolution. I am not a judge or an arbitrator. I am also not here in a representative capacity. I expect that both of you are able to speak for yourselves and make your own informed decisions.

"As we work together, I am going to do my very best to be balanced and neutral. I want to ensure that this process is fair. My taking sides will not help me and I really have no reason to do so. However, if for any reason you feel that I am taking sides, please let me know. There may be something that I can do to address your concerns. However, if there is nothing I can do, we will need to find a replacement mediator. It is more important that you mediate than that you mediate with me.

"To encourage candid and open communication, this mediation process is confidential. What you share here will not be repeated or used against you. I will not be writing a report or discussing the mediation with anyone.

"As you heard, Bill is involved and wants to support your process. He will want to see any agreements you work out. I hope you see that this is on a need-to-know basis.

"In a moment we will sign the Agreement to Mediate. It provides certain exceptions. For example, I am required to report any information that reveals criminal activity, or elder or child abuse.

"At a practical level, I wonder if either of you will in the normal course want to debrief in confidence with someone close, such as your spouse/partner or mentor. I believe it is better to acknowledge this as a reality, and to limit such disclosures to these persons. Do either of you have anyone in mind?

"At times, it may make sense for me to meet in private with each of you. We call this a caucus session. I may suggest one, and either of you are welcome to do the same.

"If we do caucus, I will not repeat what you share with me. I will make certain at the end of the private meeting exactly what I may convey to the other, if anything. I will honor your confidences. If I meet with one of you, I will meet with the other too. The same rules will apply. I will hold in confidence whatever is shared.

"Before we get started, let us consider ground rules. We know the session will be confidential. What other agreements would you like to reach that indicate how we are going to communicate with one another? What is important is that you both feel safe and comfortable. I want to be sensitive to your communication norms. For example, in some cultures, interrupting is a way of showing we are engaged. People from other cultures consider this rude, and prefer to speak in turns. I share this as an example. How will we deal with interruptions? And what other agreements are important to each of you?

"As you know, we have set aside two hours for this session. I am hopeful that we will be able to work something out in that time. However, if we are not able to do so, we can arrange another date and time at the end of this session.

"You both know where the restrooms are.

"I have been doing a lot of talking. All of this information can be overwhelming. What questions do you have at this time?"

You answer any questions.

"Now that I have answered your questions, it appears that you both understand what mediation is and want to mediate with me. Is that correct? Are we ready to begin?

"Let us take a moment to review and sign the Agreement to Mediate. It establishes the confidentiality of the proceedings and also confirms what I have been telling you about the mediation process.

The mediator, the participants and Bill sign.

Bill: "This is a great opportunity. We believe in you both and know you will do your best. I am looking forward to hearing how it goes."

"Thanks Bill!"

Bill then leaves.

"Now we can get started. Sally, are you ready to share your perspective?"

The education phase

Sally goes first. She says: "Thank you for the opportunity. This has been difficult and I have given it a lot of thought. The bottom line is that I want the performance review changed. I just cannot see how it is justified. I have never received a 2 for anything in the ten years that I have worked for Harry. I am really interested to hear what Harry has to say. As far as I am concerned, I am a good team player, always have been, and always will be. I also take pride in how I communicate.

"It is hard to accept this, as I feel what Harry did at a recent meeting was a good example of poor communication and teamwork. We were having our regular team meeting and taking turns to provide updates. Everyone had shared except me. But when it was my turn and I was ready to begin, Harry suddenly announced that he had to leave, and the meeting ended. Just like that. I could not believe it. I was so angry. And, unlike Harry, I never throw temper tantrums. So I just absorbed it. But why? It is unfair. And then, my performance review...

"To show how adamant I was that something be done, I contacted HR. That is why we are here today. I also want you to know that I have contacted the Equal Employment Opportunity (EEO) Compliance Office and am ready to file a complaint of discrimination."

Now you summarize what Sally has said, and set the stage for Harry.

You: *"Thank you for sharing so candidly, Sally. I can see that this has been very upsetting for you. You feel that the performance review is unfair and is consistent with a pattern. As an example, you described what happened at the recent meeting that ended abruptly, at least from your perspective. In fact, you are so frustrated with the situation that you are contemplating filing a complaint.*

"What I also heard was that you want to work things out. You take pride in your communication abilities and are motivated to be a team player. Importantly, you want to be included and have a fair chance at participation. How does that sound?"

After you have established that Sally is satisfied that she has been heard, you clear the table for Harry and grant him the same courtesy, that is, your open attitude.

Harry: "I did not realize you had such strong feelings. An EEO complaint. Wow! You know there is no basis for that. And, as far as I am concerned, the performance review is fair. I told you, if you dropped the ball on our standing meetings again there would be consequences. What did you think I meant?"

Sally blurts out the mediation's first interruption: "Not this. You know I do not deserve it. You are just being punitive, and if you do not budge, neither will I."

You respond: *"Harry, please continue…"*

Harry: "Thanks. Well, what I know is that we have to address this issue. I feel helpless sometimes. It is as if you just do things your own way. We agreed to meet every second week, and yet you have kept avoiding these meetings. The other thing that bothers me, which is often a result of us not meeting, is that I am not being informed about the projects you are working on. I am tired of being embarrassed because I do not know what is going on in my own department.

"You are right about the meeting. It did end abruptly, and I did not realize that you had not yet had a chance to contribute. I am sorry, I would also be upset if I were you. I suddenly remembered that I had forgotten to make a call before my meeting with the CEO. So I panicked and acted impulsively. I am sorry about that."

You: *"Thanks, Harry. So you want to have regular, one-on-one meetings with Sally, and be informed about the projects she is working on?"*

Harry: "Exactly. Is that too much to ask?"

You: *"That is what we are here to explore. And I also wanted to acknowledge that your inability to tie down the one-on-one meetings is extremely frustrating. I get the impression that this is a long-standing source of irritation."*

Harry: "Exactly. And it has to stop. I cannot go on this way. I don't understand why Sally is so resistant."

Sally: "Well, if you must know, I don't think they are necessary. If I need your input, I can just ask. The team meetings are enough, when you give me a chance to speak. There is also e-mail. And, although I have not always done so in the past, lately I have been very careful to copy you in on my e-mails. I still feel bad about that time when I did not, and you were caught off guard in that meeting."

You: *"Both of you have acknowledged things that you did that impacted one another negatively. Harry, you have apologized for what happened in the meeting. And Sally, you have apologized for what happened when Harry was not copied in on your e-mail. I am encouraged, as these apologies tell me you want to work something out. They signal your good intentions."*

Sally: "We still have to sort out the performance review rating."

Harry: "There is something else."

Sally: "Actually, I have something more too."

You: *"Harry, we still have not heard your perspective on the one-on-one meetings. Sally feels they are unnecessary."*

Harry: "I do not agree, and I am Sally's manager."

Sally: "So it is going to be a power play. So typical of you males! The minute a woman shows promise, you are threatened and move to shut her down. As far as I am concerned, if the review stands, I am going to go ahead and file my complaint of gender discrimination. Then you can see how that feels."

You: *"One possibility is for us to end this meeting without you working something out. You have to decide what is in your best interests. If I may, I would like to point out the progress you have made. The fact is, you are being real with one another. The truth is that your relationship has been under strain and you both have strong feelings about why that is so. Today you have an opportunity to clear the air, get things off your chest, apologize – as you have both already done – and decide the best way forward."*

Harry: "Filing a complaint is not going to help anyone. You know that I do not discriminate. I want to work something out. I also want to get to the bottom of things."

Harry turns towards Sally and says: "At the end of the day, I do not want to meet just for the sake of meeting. The reason I like the one-on-one meetings is that they reduce the number of times you drop in to see me. Honestly, that drives me crazy. As far as is possible, I like to plan my work day. I wish you would not assume that I always have time to see you."

Sally: "I had no idea. You are normally so direct. Why did you not tell me?"

Harry: "You may think this is strange, but I remember early on you told me about your father, and how he was not available for you; in fact, he left you out of things."

Sally: "It was so unfair. I would want to watch the football but had to work in the kitchen with my mother. Even chess was just for boys. I appreciate that we are talking now. And I am starting to feel like we can figure something out. And really, I can handle not dropping in. But in truth, I am sometimes scared when you get angry. Not just at me, but at others too. I will always remember the first time you lost your temper. I really do not like that. My family was so passive. I do not think I ever saw my parents display anger."

Harry: "You know, this is so embarrassing. I wish it was not like this. I know I do it and I am working on it. And when I lose my temper, I just have to hope and pray that I do not hurt anyone. Though I always seem to."

You: *"Harry, I see your courage in taking responsibility for this pattern of behavior. What was your family like in this respect? I have a feeling it was not like Sally's."*

Harry: "My father was a good man, of his time. His father was strict with him. He would joke that he was an Irishman with a short fuse. But in truth, I was scared of him, and that is why I hate seeing myself behaving the same way. When he was angry, he used to shout or just say mean things. Not to me alone, but in front of my friends. That was so embarrassing."

Sally: "That must have been terrible for you. I see you struggle with it. I know you do not mean to treat me badly, but it is hard. And you probably are not going to like hearing this, but you also berate me in front of others. The funny thing is that just knowing more about your past, and imagining you as that young boy, makes it easier. I know you mean well. And I sometimes wonder about myself. It seems as if we all have these massive blind spots. Thank you for being so revealing."

Harry: "Wow, this is really choking me up. Thank you."

You: *"Being vulnerable with each other is a classic way to build trust. What I can see is that you both care about one another and do want to work something out. I wonder if there is any feedback you can give, Sally? It seems, unless I am wrong, that you were asking…"*

Sally: "Yes, I would just as soon know."

Harry: "It is nothing, really. And I do not want to say anything that undermines what we have already accomplished. I suppose I sometimes think that your forgetting meetings, or not copying me in on e-mails, is passive-aggressive. I hope my saying that does not offend you."

Sally: "Ouch! Really, I do not see it that way. How can forgetting be regarded as passive-aggressive?"

Harry: "I once went on a conflict-resolution skills training course. The trainer said that if one was avoidant, one had to watch out for suppressing conflict that would later manifest as passive-aggressive behavior, like forgetting meetings. It stuck with me."

Sally: "This is so hard. But now that I think about it… that last meeting I honestly could not make. I was going to reschedule it, but then you went off at the deep end about the report being out a day late. Wow, this is so embarrassing."

You: *"Let me see if I can summarize things. My sense is that you have both been courageous and have taken as much responsibility as possible for your behavior. I am impressed.*

"It seems that there are a number of issues that we may want to take some more time exploring in full. They include the performance

review, the one-on-one meetings, project updates, and Sally's access to Harry. In addition, you both shared about how you manage your emotions when triggered. It is very common for us to use a protective strategy that is sourced from our early family experiences. How you both work on your issues and take responsibility for your feelings and behavior is going to make a huge difference. How you both support one another with compassion and understanding can transform your relationship.

"Let's spend a little more time clarifying what is important to each of you in respect of each of these issues. I would like to chart each of your needs before we move on to the option-generation phase."

Needs

Sally	Harry
• Fairness	• Performance
• Respect and recognition	• Information
• Understanding	• Good reputation
• Access	• Efficiency
• Information	• Being well regarded
• Good communication	• Privacy
• Good relationship with Harry	• Accountability
• Stress-free work environment	• Communication
• Safety	• Respect and recognition
• Care	
• Job security	

Sally: "I am encouraged that we can both admit that we have challenges. I know you are my boss. I want to respect that. Sorry if it does not always come across that way. Now that I know what you need and how you would like to be treated, I think we can work something out. What was the first issue?"

You: *"The performance review."*

Harry: "Well, if we can work something out and agree to let bygones be bygones and really get a fresh start, knowing that we are both going to do our best, then I would be willing to recommend to Bill that it be changed. But Sally, you would have to agree not to file your complaint."

The option-generation phase

You: *"We have transitioned to the option-generation phase. Now is your opportunity to come up with potential solutions that will work for both of you. To summarize, it seems that Sally needs opportunity, understanding, access, information, fairness, good communication, a sound reputation, a good relationship with Harry, a stress-free work environment, respect, recognition, safety, care and job security. Harry needs performance, information, a good reputation, efficiency, being well regarded, privacy, accountability, communication, respect and recognition. Your challenge is to meet all your needs in the best, most creative way possible.*

"Let's take the issues one at a time. This is our list:
- *The performance review*
- *The one-on-one meetings*
- *The project updates*
- *Sally's access to Harry*

"Based on what you said, Harry, I think we should perhaps end with the performance review. I am wondering if it would be helpful to consider communication in general. Or your relationship? I don't know, what do you think?"

Sally: "Let's begin with our relationship. That is the most important issue."

Harry: "I appreciate that, Sally. I don't know quite how we got here. I know this is not what I want. With some care and effort, I think we can work together better. We know one another pretty well by now. And I am encouraged that we are both trying. I get a lot of feedback due to the fact that I show my anger. It frustrates me that the avoidant types are not also held to account. Anyway, I am willing."

Sally: "You are right. I am only just starting to see how my not expressing what I really feel does not serve me well. I later resent you and chastise myself. I want to speak up for myself and not have to worry that you are going to bite my head off."

You: *"So, it sounds like we have your relationship as another issue."*

Harry: "You know, the other issues – apart from our relationship – are really all about communication. So that we each have the information we need to make decisions and do our jobs. For the most part, we are good. I suppose the one-on-one meetings are only one way I can be informed. You having free access to my office is another way. Are there other ways we could do this? The same goes for the project updates."

Sally: "I feel so much lighter. Let me see, we could review all open projects and agree on communication levels. And then, as new projects come in, we could do that from the start. I am thinking that e-mail should be the backbone, but that we will also be able to use the cloud for common access. Technology is making it so much easier to communicate. I am glad we are both on board with that."

Harry: "Yes, I actually prefer e-mails. I find it difficult to regain my focus after people drop in, and you are not the only one who does it. I struggle with that."

Sally: "What if you closed your door at certain times of the day and put up a *Busy* sign? If people need to discuss things urgently, they could come to see me. I would be happy to shield you more from drop-ins. And please don't worry about me and my father. I really have made peace with him. He meant well, he was just a man of his time, like your father was."

You: *"What were you thinking would help your relationship?"*

Harry: "That we are both committed to a more friendly one, and that we will try and show some more 'love and understanding'. Just kidding! But seriously, I think the stuff we shared about our childhoods and how we are both doing our best, given what we experienced, should find a way in."

Sally: "Harry, I agree with everything you just said. Please do not take this the wrong way, but I am wondering whether, from a practical point of view, I could take time-out when you get angry?"

Harry: "And if you do barge in on me, how can I say 'not now'?"

The negotiation phase

You: *"It seems there are many viable solutions available to consider. Some need to be discussed in more detail."*

Harry: "Like what?"

You: *"Well, you have not reached a final agreement on the performance review."*

Harry: "As far as I am concerned, it should be changed to a 4. That is, of course, if I can still do it."

You: *"Yes, you can, as long as Bill confirms your recommendation. I have some sample language that I could put into a draft agreement."*

Sally: "Thanks Harry, that means a lot to me. I suppose you also have some sample language to state that I will not file an EEO complaint. I am sorry, Harry. I know that I hurt you by mentioning it as a possibility."

Harry: "Yes, I was hurt. I really hope we can make a go of this, Sally. In the scheme of things, our lives are good. We do not need this strife."

You: *"You are right, especially when you contrast the benefits of the agreement you are working out with what the alternative scenarios look like. Most seem bleak, wouldn't you say?"*

Sally: "What do you mean?"

You: *"Well, what will you do if you do not work something out today?"*

Sally: "I would appeal the performance review decision to Bill, and if he did not change it, I would go ahead with my complaint."

You: *"Exactly! When you consider the time spent, the emotional tension, the uncertainty, and the fact that winning a complaint is not going to address any of your other issues, including the need to relate to one another, then you will appreciate that it would be better to reach an agreement. I mean, as I understand it, you are both committing to a good, healthy and mutually supportive relationship, with a workable plan of action to address your communication challenges."*

Harry: "This is great. I am sold! But guys, we have work to do."

You: *"Yes, you are right, Harry. There is work to be done. And you are still not quite done. What about the one-on-one meetings? Where did we end up on that?"*

Sally looks to Harry, and Harry says: "We do not have to meet for the sake of it. Our goal is to have good communication and both be up-to-date and informed about what we need to know. What about meeting once a month, and seeing how that goes? I like the idea of a regular, face-to-face check-in, especially if you are not going to be dropping in as much as you have been in the past."

Sally: "That sounds sensible. I will take responsibility for setting up our meetings, although I think if one of us cannot make the meeting, that person should be responsible for rescheduling."

Harry: "Sounds perfect to me!"

Closing

You: *"There are a couple of clauses I would encourage you to consider. One is an agreement that I can follow up with you in about six weeks' time. It is considered sensible. The other is that you think about who you want to share this agreement with. Apart from Bill, is there anyone who needs to know? What I will do is draft an agreement and run it by you both. Once we are settled on the terms, I will schedule a meeting with Bill so he can witness your signatures. He will be happy with your good work. As other people may be curious, you could consider what I call a 'press release' clause, which is a phrase you both agree to use if asked about the mediation. For instance: 'Thanks for asking. Yes, we did mediate. It worked out well. I am not at liberty to say more.'"*

Sally: "Thanks Harry. I think we can work better together. I know I am going to do my best."

Harry: "Me too. I am also optimistic about things!"

Harry and Sally turn to you.

Harry: "Thanks! This was not exactly what I had expected, but I sure am happy with the way it worked out."

Sally: "It is as if we have brought some peace to work!"

You: *"That is what I imagine every day! I hope that when we meet again in six weeks' time, things will be going well."*

As the mediator, you now document the agreement. Appendix 5 on page 167 gives a sample agreement drafted for the fictitious Harry and Sally. The clauses are tailored for the example mediation given here. Also included are some other possible clauses, to give you a sense of what can be articulated in an agreement of this nature.

I hope this chapter has given you a feel for how a mediation session can unfold; a sense of the process. Obviously, some of the conversations would need to be fleshed out more, especially regarding how Harry and Sally would relate to each other in the future. And, of course, an actual mediation session will take a lot longer than the time it took you to read this chapter.

Chapter 13
Peace at Work

"Peace is not the absence of conflict but the presence of creative alternatives for responding to conflict – alternatives to passive or aggressive responses, alternatives to violence."
Dorothy Thompson

Given the inevitability of conflict and disputes, fair questions to ask are: How well are we as HR professionals doing at resolving conflict at our places of work? Is it easy for employees to raise issues, debate ideas, and resolve conflicts around behavior and treatment? How skilled are employees at resolving conflicts once issues have been raised? And when they get stuck, what are the process options? Is mediation being offered?

My optimism motivated me to write this book. My hope has always been to inspire others to turn towards, rather than away from, the conflicts in their lives. Mostly simply, mediation involves a third person helping two others to resolve their differences themselves. It is not new. We, however, are the new generation with the responsibility for resolving the conflicts and disputes of our times.

Mediation is increasingly being seen as a viable conflict-resolution option. Private companies, universities, government departments, courts, and private citizens are recognizing that the power-based ways of old no longer serve us. Mediation limits the use of power and is therefore a move in the right direction. We also have to get beyond simplistic 'right and wrong' thinking, and structure our solutions around meeting everyone's needs in the most creative and fair way possible.

You have an opportunity to be part of the shift that is emerging in the world; by taking responsibility; by simply saying: "Yes, we can!"

As we have discovered, we now know a lot more about conflict and how we can resolve it, both through external processes like negotiation, and through internal and more reflective practices like forgive-

157

ness. I have no doubt that we will continue to see the emergence of new, evidence-based research that supports our understanding of how best to intervene in conflicts.

The value proposition for the use of mediation for employment disputes external to organizations has already been established. Certainly, here in the United States, for the courts and both the Federal and State enforcement agencies, mediation has become the default way to resolve disputes. The challenge for the future is to bring mediation in-house. If mediation makes sense for disputes that have left the organization, it makes more sense to mediate while they are still within it. In fact, the theory is that addressing conflict at the earliest opportunity is always the best way, and that the use of needs-based, collaborative procedures like mediation makes perfect sense.

In time, mediation will become part of the way we do business. We will find provisions in employee handbooks, just like we do for investigations. Employees will come to expect mediation as an option. Employee-relations specialists will be competent in the conduct of both investigations and mediations. For many of you, the first step will be to increase the use of mediation, even if on an *ad hoc* basis. The materials included in the appendices will hopefully help to get you started.

You are that inspired leader who has a sense of the future, and whose time has come! I hope this book has increased your confidence in your own ability to support others to reach agreement, not just superficially, but in a real and lasting manner.

Many of you are already mediating, even if intuitively. I hope this book has helped you to learn something new, and that you have gained some comfort from knowing that what you have intuitively started doing has a name – mediation – and is fast establishing itself as a dependable workplace peace process.

Good luck!
John Ford

Appendix 1
Agreements to Mediate

1. Agreement to Mediate (Example 1)[1]

I am participating in mediation to see if it will be possible to enhance communication and/or resolve pending issues or problems. I understand and agree to the following terms and conditions regarding the mediation process:

1. I understand that mediation is a conciliatory process in which an acceptable third party intervenes in the conflict or dispute between participants to support them to reach agreement.
2. Mediation is voluntary and with prior notice to the mediator I can withdraw at any time. I understand that any agreement reached during mediation is entirely voluntary.
3. I understand that the mediator's role is not to decide who is right or wrong, or who wins or loses. Rather, the mediator will facilitate communication to assist us, the participants, to reach our own mutually acceptable resolution of this matter.
4. I understand that the mediator is not going to act as an advocate or representative for me or for anyone else.
5. I understand that mediation is a confidential process and I agree to respect the confidentiality of all discussions and communications made during or in connection with the mediation. I understand that the purpose of mediation is to try to improve communication and/or resolve a conflict or dispute, and not to gather information for other purposes.
6. I understand that the mediator will not voluntarily testify on behalf of any participant and will not report anything said during this mediation *unless* one of the participants makes a genuine threat of physical harm or reveals information of criminal activity, child abuse or elder abuse.
7. I agree that I will not subpoena the mediator, or any other persons participating in the mediation, to testify about anything that was said or written down during or in connection with the mediation.

8. It is the intention that all confidentiality protections afforded by law apply to each mediation. To preserve the confidentiality of the mediation process, I understand and agree that if I raise claims in this mediation that, if true, would constitute a violation of Company policy or law, my raising of any such claims does not constitute notice to the Company of such violations. In order to report claims alleging a violation of Company policy or law, I will follow appropriate internal Company procedures for the reporting of such claims.

9. This *Agreement to Mediate* itself is not confidential.

Date: _____

Name: _____

Name: _____

Mediator: _____

2. Agreement to Mediate (Example 2)[2]

1. The parties agree to try to resolve this case through mediation. The parties understand that settlement during mediation is entirely voluntary.

2. The parties understand that the mediator has no power to decide who wins or loses this case and will not express an opinion on who is right or wrong. Rather, the mediator will try to help the parties to reach their own resolution of this case by facilitating the discussion.

3. The parties understand that the mediator is not going to act as an advocate or attorney for any participant and that each party has the right to have a representative during mediation.

4. The parties understand that the purpose of mediation is to explore whether the parties can reach a resolution, not to gather information for a hearing or trial. The parties agree not to subpoena the mediator or any observer to testify about what was said in mediation.

5. The mediator and all observers agree not to voluntarily testify on behalf of any party and will not report anything said during this mediation *unless* one of the participants makes a genuine threat of physical harm or reveals information of criminal activity, fraud, waste, abuse of postal property, sexual harassment, child abuse or elder abuse.
6. The mediation session will not be recorded by anyone (either by video or in audio format) and no transcript of the session will be produced.
7. The parties understand that any documents prepared for or during mediation (such as case summaries presented to the mediator, or notes taken by the mediator) are for settlement purposes only and may not be subpoenaed for, or used in, a hearing or trial. Documents that existed before mediation are *not* shielded from later use or disclosure just because they were discussed or used in mediation.
8. The parties understand that no participant will be bound by anything said or done in mediation unless and until there is a written settlement agreement.

Date: _____

Participant: _____

Representative: _____

Participant: _____

Representative: _____

Mediator: _____

Observer: _____

---

[1] Adapted from the UCSF Mediation Program.
[2] Adapted from the United States Postal Service.

Appendix 2

Ground Rules for Mediation[1]

1. We will take turns speaking and not interrupt each other.
2. We will remain focused on the issues at hand and avoid being sidetracked into other non-relevant areas.
3. We will not demean, belittle, blame or attack each other, nor will we engage in put-downs, and will ask questions of each other for the purposes of gaining clarity and understanding only.
4. We will stay away from establishing hard positions and express ourselves in terms of our personal needs and the outcomes we wish to realize.
5. We will listen respectfully, and sincerely try to understand the other person's needs. We will not make assumptions about the other person's motives or needs.
6. We recognize that even if we do not agree with the other person's perspective, each of us is entitled to our own perspective.
7. We will not dwell on things that did not work in the past but instead will focus on the future we would like to create.
8. We will make a conscious, sincere effort to refrain from unproductive arguing, venting and defensiveness.
9. We agree to work hard towards what we perceive to be the fairest and most creative agreement possible.
10. We will speak up if something is not working for us in mediation. In particular, we will point out if we feel the mediator is not being balanced.

---

[1] Adapted with the permission of Jim Melamed.

Appendix 3: Needs Inventory

Substantive Topic/Issue	Relationship Dynamics	Identity/Reputation	Process Concerns
What do I want?	What do we need to relate to one another?	How do I want to be seen?	What is important about the process?
Accuracy	Acceptance	Adventurous	Balance
Assignments	Accountability	Authoritative	Certainty
Benefits	Acknowledgement	Caring	Clarity
Change	Affection	Compassionate	Clarity of decision-making rules
Compliance	Appreciation	Competent	Confidentiality
Competence	Approval	Considerate	Consistency
Consideration	Apology	Consistent	Disclosure
Contribution	Authenticity	Creative	Efficiency
Creativity	Autonomy	Dependable	Equal airtime
Customer satisfaction	Belonging	Serious	Equal treatment
Efficiency	Care	Ethical	Equality
Equality	Comfort	Expert	Fairness
Equipment	Commitment	Fair	Honesty
Expectations	Communication	Friendly	Involvement
Freedom	Compassion	Fun	Notification
Health	Conciliation	Generous	Opportunity to speak
Information	Connection	Harmonious	Participation
Job security	Control	Honest	Precedent
Lawful treatment	Ease	Inspiring	Privacy
Learning	Empathy	Integritous	Punctuality
Money	Fair treatment	Intelligent	Safety
Office location	Forgiveness	Kind	Timeliness
Peace	Friendship	Lawful	Trust
Performance	Fun	Leader	
	Help	Logical	
	Honesty	Nurturing	
Productivity	Hope	Organized	
Promotion	Inclusion	Peaceful	
Protection	Independence	Powerful	
Purpose	Inspiration	Reasonable	
Quality work	Integrity	Reliable	
Relationship	Intimacy	Reputable	
Roles	Love	Responsible	
Safety	Loyalty	Sensitive	
Salary/Money	Meaning	Strong	
Saving face	Morale	Thoughtful	
Security	Motivation	Trusting	
Structure	Mourning	Victim	
Time	Power	Well-regarded	
Title	Predictability		
Training	Privacy		
Trust	Reassurance		
	Recognition		
	Reliability		
	Respect		
	Saving face		
	Security		
	Shared reality		
	Support		
	Trust		
	Understanding		
	Vindication		

Appendix 4
Guide to Emotions

Paul Ekman, a psychologist from the University of California, San Francisco (UCSF), established the universality of facial expressions and identified seven core emotions that all humans are hardwired to display: anger, fear, sadness, contempt, disgust, happiness and surprise.[1]

Mediators need to recognize the different emotions and decide how they influence the decision-making process in a mediation. They need to tune into and sense the emotional states of the participants. Not only does the mediator need to recognize each participant's emotional state (let's say, for instance, anger or sadness), but also the intensity of the emotion (how angry or how sad the person is).

It is worth remembering that there is nothing wrong with any emotion. Emotions convey information about how we experience something. This is vital decision-making information, without which we are rudderless. And, as psychologist John Gottman has discovered with his pioneering evidence-based work with conflicting couples in his Love Lab, the display of negative emotions is not the issue, provided the negative-to-positive ratio is at least 5 to 1. However, what is vital is that there is no 'negative affect reciprocity'. This is how Gottman describes it:

> *"This term refers to the increased probability that a person's emotions will be negative (anger, belligerence, sadness, contempt, and so on) right after his or her partner has exhibited negativity... Negative affect reciprocity has been the most consistent discriminator between happily and unhappily married couples."*[2]

Anger arises when someone or something is interfering with the attainment of our actual or expected needs. There is a sense of being powerless about a situation. It feels intense and is naturally energizing in the heat of the moment. As a result, it burns a lot of energy and is ultimately tiring.

Anger often begins mildly, as irritation, then grows to frustration and then to anger and rage. When we are angry, we may raise our voices, use a harsh tone, lash out, or seek to inflict pain. We tend to make impulsive and premature decisions.

Fear is designed to guard us against danger and loss, whether physical or psychological. We are afraid of physical harm, and we worry that we will lose what we have – whether it be something tangible, like our home or job, or something linked to our identities, like our good reputations. We often create fear by imagining things to worry about.

We can think about fear as a program that can be applied to any situation we want to ward against. Fear alerts us to remove ourselves from the dangerous situation and to apply protective strategies. Sometimes, if the fear is sudden or severe, we tend to freeze and are unable to function or retrieve data. We get that 'deer in the headlights' look. When fear is driven by thoughts of the uncertain future, it can produce a relentless, restless, self-occupied state. With fear, as with anger, there tends to be a continuum – anxiety leads to worry, worry leads to fear, fear leads to terror. People who are afraid often tend to cower and/or struggle to make decisions, in part because of their inability to focus on what is possible.

Sadness conveys a powerful sense of loss. Something is gone. In the moment of grief it is usually debilitating. Things literally slow down (energetically speaking). People in mourning are often lethargic and lack energy.

When we are sad we tend to withdraw. With sadness too there can be a continuum – we are upset, then disappointed, then sad, and finally devastated. As with fear, we are cautious about making decisions.

Contempt can be viewed as a combination of anger and disgust. Contempt is the disdain we have for another's action, words or ideas. Contempt tends to make us arrogant and give us a sense of superiority so that we are often tempted to ridicule and insult people. Contempt also tends to make us intensely focused, and possibly punitive.

Contempt is a particularly toxic emotion and signals strong dislike. Like surprise, there is no continuum – contempt is contempt. Sometimes, people mistake contempt for happiness. It is difficult and unwise to make a decision when one is feeling contempt.

Disgust manifests when we dislike something intensely. In a social sense, it is used to convey displeasure with another's behavior. Disgust is used to show that we do not want to associate with someone's behavior, or that we want to distance ourselves from it. Loathing is an even stronger form of disgust. In circumstances where one feels disgust, the tendency is to rush decisions so that one can remove oneself from the situation.

Surprise goes hand in hand with other emotions. Surprise is often the first emotion to manifest, and by definition is fleeting. For instance, we are surprised to hear about a raise in pay, then quickly transition to gladness. Or we are surprised to hear that our benefits have changed for the worse, then quickly transition to anger that there is nothing we can do about it. We are surprised by that which we do not know. When the uncertainty is not resolved quickly, a surprised state can be debilitating as we await the good or bad news.

Surprise is often a very intense emotion, whether it be amazement, awe or shock. Due to this intensity, it is difficult to make decisions in a state of surprise.

Happiness is a sign that we have what we believe we need. We are engaged, energized, optimistic and ready to move forward. When we are genuinely happy, we smile and our whole face lights up, especially our eyes, which is a different thing to pulling back the corners of our mouths in a socially acceptable but unauthentic 'smile'.

The happiness spectrum starts with satisfaction, moves through happiness, and ends with joy. Decisions are easily made in a state of happiness; in fact, one has to be conscious of being over-optimistic.

---

[1]   Ekman, 2003.
[2]   Gottman, 1999:37.

Appendix 5

Settlement Agreement of Harry and Sally

Harry and Sally have taken the time to reach new understandings about the 2010 performance review, and how they can improve their professional working relationship with one another. This agreement addresses the performance review issue, and documents how their agreement will be implemented. It also puts the past to rest, and sets forth the points of their understanding for working productively together in the future.

***

Commitment to relationship
We are committed to a productive and professional working relationship that advances the shared goals of our department. We agree to show each other respect in our communications and to act in a courteous, professional and responsible manner.

Commitment to communicate
We acknowledge that clear communication is important for a healthy relationship. We will be direct, concise and focused in our communication. We will use the variety of communication and online tools available to most effectively stay informed about our work projects.

To support clear communication, we agree to listen to one another with the goal of us both being heard and understood. We will reflect back to one another what was said (the feelings, thoughts and needs) in a way that is supportive to the speaker. Reflecting back does not mean that we are agreeing with one another.

Performance review
Harry agrees to recommend to the Director of Operations to formally change the end-of-year performance rating of Sally from a 2 to a 4

with respect to the Communication and Teamwork standard. This change will be made within two weeks of the approval of the Director of Operations. It will be effective from the date of the original performance review. The change will be reflected in Sally's formal personnel file held by HR in the company's Head Office in San Francisco, CA.

If Sally believes that the Company has not complied with any terms or conditions of this agreement, Sally will notify in writing the Director of Human Resources concerning the alleged non-compliance within 30 days of when she knew or should have known of the alleged non-compliance. Sally may request that the terms of this agreement be specifically implemented or, alternatively, that the complaint be reinstated for further processing from the point that processing ceased.

EEO complaint
Subject to the above, Sally agrees not to file a claim that she was discriminated against on the basis of her gender when given an annual performance rating of 2 in respect of Communication and Teamwork in 2010.

Project updates
Sally will keep Harry informed and up-to-date regarding all the projects on which she is working. She will use the monthly meeting and e-mail as her primary means of informing Harry.

Monthly one-on-one meetings
We agree to a bi-monthly check-in meeting with one another. Sally will be responsible for scheduling the meeting. If the meeting needs to be postponed, the person requesting the postponement will be responsible for rescheduling the meeting and for confirming such arrangements in writing. We will review, on an ongoing basis, the efficacy of these meetings and make improvements to this arrangement, if warranted.

Access and drop-in protocol
Sally will respect Harry's need for productive working time without interruption, and understands the negative impact of drop-ins on

Harry with regard to his concentration and focus. Sally will manage her communication with Harry in a way that minimizes drop-ins, and will also monitor and intercept other people who disturb Harry in this way, with the aim of trying to help them with their issues. We understand that there will invariably be 'drop everything' requests, but that, in general, we will be respectful of one another's activities.

Time-outs

We agree that if either of us indicates the need for a 'time-out' the other will honor it. The person who requests the 'time-out' will call the 'time-in' to reopen the discussion of the issue within 24 hours.

Triggers and response strategies

We will both strive not to take things personally. To the extent that we are triggered and are aware of our emotional 'charge', we will have the courage to speak to each other as soon as possible, and at a time that allows us both to be at our best.

We agree to let one another know when we are triggered, and why, without using judgmental language. We will try to follow the spirit of the following 'I Statement' formula:
- I feel {describe feeling}
- When {describe behavior in neutral terms}
- Because {describe impact on needs}
- I would appreciate/prefer/Could we {make positive behavior change}

Recognize and respect different styles

We acknowledge that we have different styles and will both work to be respectful of our differences.

Future disagreements

We agree that if we have concerns, suggestions or questions about an issue relating to one another, we will talk privately and in confidence with one another. If we cannot reach agreement on an issue on our own, we will look to the Director of Operations for support and guidance.

Confidentiality

The confidentiality of the mediation process will be respected. We are comfortable sharing this agreement with the Director of Operations. If others ask about the mediation, we will respond using the following words: "Thanks for asking. We participated in a mediation session and worked something out in private."

Follow-up

The mediator will meet with Sally and Harry about six weeks after the date of signature of this agreement, and again as needed, to establish how things are going and to provide support for the success of this relationship.

Date: _____

_____
Sally

_____
Harry

Witnessed by Management and Mediator:

_____
Director of Operations

_____
Mediator

Appendix 6
Sample Mediation Participant Survey

TO BE COMPLETED BY THE MEDIATION PARTICIPANTS

Please complete this form promptly after the mediation and return it via inter-office mail to: _____

If you have any additional comments on your mediation experience, or suggestions on how to improve the mediation process, please use additional sheets.

Thank you.

***

Name of mediator: _____

Date of mediation: _____

Complainant's name: _____

Are you the: ☐ Complainant ☐ Respondent

Have you received training regarding the mediation process, its goals and benefits?
☐ Yes ☐ No

Have you participated in mediation before?
☐ Yes ☐ No

Was the time and place scheduled for the mediation session convenient for you?
☐ Yes ☐ No

Was the mediation process an appropriate way to resolve your dispute?

☐ Yes ☐ No

Did you reach an agreement to settle your dispute?

☐ Yes ☐ No

If you reached an agreement to settle, do you consider it to be fair?

☐ Yes ☐ No

Would you use mediation again?

☐ Yes ☐ No

Please circle the number which best reflects how you feel about the following statements:

Strongly agree (1); Agree (2); Not sure (3); Disagree (4); Strongly disagree (5)

1. The amount of time spent in mediation was appropriate.

   1   2   3   4   5

2. The information I received about the mediation process was appropriate.

   1   2   3   4   5

3. The mediator allowed me to fully present information and my side of the dispute.

   1   2   3   4   5

4. I fully understood what was going on at all times during the mediation.

   1   2   3   4   5

5. The mediation changed my opinion of the other person for the better.

   1   2   3   4   5

6. Overall, I was satisfied with the mediation process.

   1   2   3   4   5

7. The mediator explained the mediation process clearly.

   1   2   3   4   5

8. The mediator effectively clarified my key issues and concerns.

   1   2   3   4   5

9. There was no pressure from the mediator to settle the dispute.

   1   2   3   4   5

10. The mediator treated all the persons fairly.

   1   2   3   4   5

11. The mediator helped to create realistic options for settling the dispute.

   1   2   3   4   5

12. The mediator understood the issues involved.

   1   2   3   4   5

13. Overall, I was satisfied with the mediator.

   1   2   3   4   5

---

[1] Adapted from the FDIC EEO Mediation Program.

Appendix 7
Model Standards of Conduct for Mediators[1]

Preamble

Mediation is used to resolve a broad range of conflicts within a variety of settings. These Standards are designed to serve as fundamental ethical guidelines for persons mediating in all practice contexts. They serve three primary goals: to guide the conduct of mediators; to inform the mediating parties; and to promote public confidence in mediation as a process for resolving disputes.

Mediation is a process in which an impartial third party facilitates communication and negotiation and promotes voluntary decision making by the parties to the dispute. Mediation serves various purposes, including providing the opportunity for parties to define and clarify issues, understand different perspectives, identify interests, explore and assess possible solutions, and reach mutually satisfactory agreements, when desired.

Note on Construction

These Standards are to be read and construed in their entirety. There is no priority significance attached to the sequence in which the Standards appear.

The use of the term 'shall' in a Standard indicates that the mediator must follow the practice described. The term 'should' indicates that the practice described in the Standard is highly desirable, but not required, and is to be departed from only for very strong reasons, and requires careful use of judgment and discretion. The term 'mediator' is understood to be inclusive so that it applies to co-mediator models.

These Standards do not include specific temporal parameters when referencing a mediation and therefore do not define the exact beginning or ending of a mediation.

Various aspects of a mediation, including some matters covered by these Standards, may also be affected by applicable law, court rules, regulations, other applicable professional rules, mediation rules to which the parties have agreed, and other agreements of the parties. These sources may create conflicts with, and may take precedence over, these Standards. However, a mediator should make every effort to comply with the spirit and intent of these Standards in resolving such conflicts. This effort should include honoring all remaining Standards not in conflict with these other sources.

These Standards, unless and until adopted by a court or other regulatory authority, do not have the force of law. Nonetheless, the fact that these Standards have been adopted by the respective sponsoring entities should alert mediators to the fact that the Standards might be viewed as establishing a standard of care for mediators.

***

STANDARD I. SELF-DETERMINATION

A. A mediator shall conduct a mediation based on the principle of party self-determination. Self-determination is the act of coming to a voluntary, uncoerced decision in which each party makes free and informed choices as to process and outcome. Parties may exercise self-determination at any stage of a mediation, including mediator selection, process design, participation in or withdrawal from the process, and outcomes.

1. Although party self-determination for process design is a fundamental principle of mediation practice, a mediator may need to balance such party self-determination with a mediator's duty to conduct a quality process in accordance with these Standards.

2. A mediator cannot personally ensure that each party has made free and informed choices to reach particular decisions, but, where appropriate, a mediator should make the parties aware of the importance of consulting other professionals to help them make informed choices.

B. A mediator shall not undermine party self-determination by any party for reasons such as higher settlement rates, egos, increased fees, or outside pressures from court personnel, program administrators, provider organizations, the media, or others.

STANDARD II. IMPARTIALITY

A. A mediator shall decline a mediation if the mediator cannot conduct it in an impartial manner. Impartiality means freedom from favoritism, bias or prejudice.

B. A mediator shall conduct a mediation in an impartial manner and avoid conduct that gives the appearance of partiality.

   1. A mediator should not act with partiality or prejudice based on any participant's personal characteristics, background, values and beliefs, or performance at a mediation, or any other reason.

   2. A mediator should neither give nor accept a gift, favor, loan or other item of value that raises a question as to the mediator's actual or perceived impartiality.

   3. A mediator may accept or give *de minimis* gifts or incidental items or services that are provided to facilitate a mediation or respect cultural norms, so long as such practices do not raise questions as to a mediator's actual or perceived impartiality.

C. If at any time a mediator is unable to conduct a mediation in an impartial manner, the mediator shall withdraw.

STANDARD III. CONFLICTS OF INTEREST

A. A mediator shall avoid a conflict of interest or the appearance of a conflict of interest during and after a mediation. A conflict of interest can arise from involvement by a mediator with the subject matter of the dispute, or from any relationship between a mediator and any mediation participant, whether past or present, personal or professional, that reasonably raises a question of a mediator's impartiality.

B. A mediator shall make a reasonable inquiry to determine whether there are any facts that a reasonable individual would consider likely to create a potential or actual conflict of interest for a mediator. A mediator's actions necessary to accomplish a reasonable inquiry into potential conflicts of interest may vary based on practice context.

C. A mediator shall disclose, as soon as practicable, all actual and potential conflicts of interest that are reasonably known to the mediator and could reasonably be seen as raising a question about the mediator's impartiality. After disclosure, if all parties agree, the mediator may proceed with the mediation.

D. If a mediator learns any fact after accepting a mediation that raises a question with respect to that mediator's service creating a potential or actual conflict of interest, the mediator shall disclose it as quickly as practicable. After disclosure, if all parties agree, the mediator may proceed with the mediation.

E. If a mediator's conflict of interest might reasonably be viewed as undermining the integrity of the mediation, the mediator shall withdraw from or decline to proceed with the mediation, regardless of the expressed desire or agreement of the parties to the contrary.

F. Subsequent to a mediation, a mediator shall not establish another relationship with any of the participants in any matter that would raise questions about the integrity of the mediation. When a mediator develops personal or professional relationships with parties, other individuals or organizations following a mediation in which the mediator was involved, the mediator should consider factors such as time elapsed following the mediation, the nature of the relationships established, and services offered, when determining whether the relationships might create a perceived or actual conflict of interest.

STANDARD IV. COMPETENCE

A. A mediator shall mediate only when the mediator has the necessary competence to satisfy the reasonable expectations of the parties.

   1. Any person may be selected as a mediator, provided that the parties are satisfied with the mediator's competence and qualifications. Training, experience in mediation, skills, cultural understandings and other qualities are often necessary for mediator competence. A person who offers to serve as a mediator creates the expectation that the person is competent to mediate effectively.

   2. A mediator should attend educational programs and related activities to maintain and enhance the mediator's knowledge and skills related to mediation.

   3. A mediator should have relevant information available for the parties relating to the mediator's training, education, experience and approach to conducting a mediation.

B. If a mediator, during the course of a mediation, determines that the mediator cannot conduct the mediation competently, the mediator shall discuss that determination with the parties as soon as is practicable and take appropriate steps to address the situation, including, but not limited to, withdrawing or requesting appropriate assistance.

C. If a mediator's ability to conduct a mediation is impaired by drugs, alcohol, medication or otherwise, the mediator shall not conduct the mediation.

STANDARD V. CONFIDENTIALITY

A. A mediator shall maintain the confidentiality of all information obtained by the mediator in mediation, unless otherwise agreed to by the parties or required by applicable law.

1. If the parties to a mediation agree that the mediator may disclose information obtained during the mediation, the mediator may do so.

2. A mediator should not communicate to any non-participant information about how the parties acted in the mediation. A mediator may report, if required, whether parties appeared at a scheduled mediation and whether or not the parties reached a resolution.

3. If a mediator participates in teaching, research or evaluation of mediation, the mediator should protect the anonymity of the parties and abide by their reasonable expectations regarding confidentiality.

B. A mediator who meets with any persons in private session during a mediation shall not convey directly or indirectly to any other person any information that was obtained during that private session without the consent of the disclosing person.

C. A mediator shall promote understanding among the parties of the extent to which the parties will maintain confidentiality of information they obtain in a mediation.

D. Depending on the circumstance of a mediation, the parties may have varying expectations regarding confidentiality that a mediator should address. The parties may make their own rules with respect to confidentiality, or the accepted practice of an individual mediator or institution may dictate a particular set of expectations.

STANDARD VI. QUALITY OF THE PROCESS

A. A mediator shall conduct a mediation in accordance with these Standards and in a manner that promotes diligence, timeliness, safety, presence of the appropriate participants, party participation, procedural fairness, party competency, and mutual respect among all participants.

1. A mediator should agree to mediate only when the mediator is prepared to commit the attention essential to an effective mediation.

2. A mediator should only accept cases when the mediator can satisfy the reasonable expectation of the parties concerning the timing of a mediation.

3. The presence or absence of persons at a mediation depends on the agreement of the parties and the mediator. The parties and mediator may agree that others may be excluded from particular sessions or from all sessions.

4. A mediator should promote honesty and candor between and among all participants, and a mediator shall not knowingly misrepresent any material fact or circumstance in the course of a mediation.

5. The role of a mediator differs substantially from other professional roles. Mixing the role of a mediator and the role of another profession is problematic, and thus a mediator should distinguish between the roles. A mediator may provide information that the mediator is qualified by training or experience to provide, only if the mediator can do so in a way that is consistent with these Standards.

6. A mediator shall not conduct a dispute-resolution procedure other than mediation but label it mediation in an effort to gain the protection of rules, statutes, or other governing authorities pertaining to mediation.

7. A mediator may recommend, when appropriate, that parties consider resolving their dispute through arbitration, counseling, neutral evaluation, or other processes.

8. A mediator shall not undertake an additional dispute-resolution role in the same matter without the consent of the parties. Before providing such service, the mediator shall inform the

parties of the implications of the change in process, and obtain their consent to the change. A mediator who undertakes such a role assumes different duties and responsibilities that may be governed by other standards.

9. If a mediation is being used to further criminal conduct, the mediator should take appropriate steps, including, if necessary, postponing, withdrawing from or terminating the mediation.

10. If a party appears to have difficulty comprehending the process, issues, or settlement options, or difficulty participating in a mediation, the mediator should explore the circumstances and potential accommodations, modifications or adjustments that would make possible the party's capacity to comprehend, participate in and exercise self-determination.

B. If a mediator is made aware of domestic abuse or violence among the parties, the mediator shall take appropriate steps, including, if necessary, postponing, withdrawing from or terminating the mediation.

C. If a mediator believes that participant conduct, including that of the mediator, jeopardizes conducting a mediation consistent with these Standards, the mediator shall take appropriate steps, including, if necessary, postponing, withdrawing from or terminating the mediation.

STANDARD VII. ADVERTISING AND SOLICITATION

A. A mediator shall be truthful and not misleading when advertising, soliciting or otherwise communicating the mediator's qualifications, experience, services and fees.

1. A mediator should not include any promises as to outcome in communications, including business cards, stationery, or computer-based communications.

2. A mediator should only claim to meet the mediator qualifications of a governmental entity or private organization if that

entity or organization has a recognized procedure for qualifying mediators and it grants such status to the mediator.

B. A mediator shall not solicit in a manner that gives an appearance of partiality for or against a party or otherwise undermines the integrity of the process.

C. A mediator shall not communicate to others, in promotional materials or through other forms of communication, the names of persons served, without their permission.

STANDARD VIII. FEES AND OTHER CHARGES

A. A mediator shall provide each party or each party's representative true and complete information about mediation fees, expenses and any other actual or potential charges that may be incurred in connection with a mediation.

1. If a mediator charges fees, the mediator should develop them in light of all relevant factors, including the type and complexity of the matter, the qualifications of the mediator, the time required, and the rates customary for such mediation services.

2. A mediator's fee arrangement should be in writing unless the parties request otherwise.

B. A mediator shall not charge fees in a manner that impairs a mediator's impartiality.

1. A mediator should not enter into a fee agreement which is contingent upon the result of the mediation or amount of the settlement.

2. While a mediator may accept unequal fee payments from the parties, the mediator should not allow such a fee arrangement to adversely impact the mediator's ability to conduct a mediation in an impartial manner.

STANDARD IX. ADVANCEMENT OF MEDIATION PRACTICE

A. A mediator should act in a manner that advances the practice of mediation. A mediator promotes this Standard by engaging in some or all of the following:

1. Fostering diversity within the field of mediation.

2. Striving to make mediation accessible to those who elect to use it, including providing services at a reduced rate or on a pro bono basis, as appropriate.

3. Participating in research when given the opportunity, including obtaining participant feedback, as appropriate.

4. Participating in outreach and education efforts to assist the public in developing an improved understanding of and appreciation for mediation.

5. Assisting newer mediators through training, mentoring and networking.

B. A mediator should demonstrate respect for differing points of view within the field, seek to learn from other mediators, and work together with other mediators to improve the profession and better serve people in conflict.

---

[1] The *Model Standards of Conduct for Mediators* was prepared in 1994 by the American Arbitration Association, the American Bar Association's Section of Dispute Resolution, and the Association for Conflict Resolution. A joint committee consisting of representatives from the same successor organizations revised the Model Standards in 2005. Both the original 1994 version and the 2005 revision have been approved by each participating organization.

Appendix 8
References

Ambady, N. et al., 'Surgeons' tone of voice: A clue to malpractice history', in: *Surgery*, Vol. 132, No. 1, 2002.

Axelrod, R., *The Evolution of Cooperation*, Basic Books, 1984.

Barker, E., *Forgiveness Workbook*, Dialogue Press, 2009.

Bennett, M. & Hermann, M., *The Art of Mediation*, NITA Publications, 1996.

Billikopf, G., *Party Directed Mediation: Helping Others Resolve Differences*, U. C. Berkeley Regents, 2nd Ed., 2009.

Brown, M., *The Presence Process*, Namaste Publishing, 2005.

Bush, R. A. B. & Folger, J. P., *The Promise of Mediation: Responding to Conflict Through Empowerment and Recognition*, Jossey-Bass, 1994.

Carpenter, S. L. & Kennedy, W. J. D., *Managing Public Disputes*, Jossey-Bass, 2nd Ed., 2001.

Chopra, D., Ford, D. & Williamson, M., *The Shadow Effect: Illuminating the Hidden Power of your True Self*, HarperCollins, 2010.

Cialdini, R. B., *Influence: The Psychology of Persuasion*, Quill, 1993.

Cloke, K. & Goldsmith, J., *Resolving Personal and Organizational Conflict: Stories of Transformation and Forgiveness*, Jossey-Bass, 2000.

Cloke, K., *Mediating Dangerously: The Frontiers of Conflict Resolution*, Jossey-Bass, 2001.

Coleman, P., *The Five Percent: Finding Solutions to Seemingly Impossible Conflicts*, PublicAffairs Books, 2011.

Covey, S. *The 90/10 Principle*, http://www.youtube.com/watch?v=6YKZmtiXnLk, 2011.

Crawley, J. & Graham, K., *Mediation for Managers: Resolving Conflict and Rebuilding Relationships at Work*, NB Publishing, 2002.

Crum, T. F., *The Magic of Conflict: Turning a Life of Work into a Work of Art*, Simon & Schuster, 1987.

Dana, D., *Managing Differences: How to Build Better Relationships at Work and Home*, MTI Publications, 2nd Ed., 1999.

Dana, D., *Conflict Resolution: Mediation Tools for Everyday Worklife*, McGraw-Hill, 2001.

De Waal, F., *Our Inner Ape: The Best and Worst of Human Nature*, Riverhead Books, 2005.

Dimasio, A., *Descartes' Error: Emotion, Reason and the Human Brain*, Quill, 2000.

Ekman, P., *Emotions Revealed: Recognizing Faces and Feelings to Improve Communication and Emotional Life*, Owl Books, 2003.

Fagan, J. & Shepherd, I. L. (Eds), *Gestalt Therapy Now: Theory, Techniques, Applications*, Science and Behavior Books, 1970.

Fisher, R., Ury, W. & Patton, B., *Getting to YES, Negotiating Agreement Without Giving In*, Penguin Books, 2nd Ed., 1991.

Gigerenzer, G., *Gut Feelings: The Intelligence of the Unconscious*, Penguin Books, 2007.

Gladwell, M., *Blink: The Power of Thinking without Thinking*, Time Warner, 2005.

Goleman, D., *Emotional Intelligence*, Bantam, 1995.

Goleman, D., Boyatzis, R. & McKee, A., *Primal Leadership: Learning to Lead with Emotional Intelligence*, Harvard Business School Press, 2002.

Gottman, J. M., *The Marriage Clinic: A Scientifically-based Marital Therapy*, Norton, 1999.

Gottman, J. M., *The Science of Trust: Emotional Attunement for Couples*, Norton, 2011.

Hiam, A., *Dealing With Conflict Instrument, Leader's Guide*, HRD Press, 1999.

Katie, B., *Loving What Is: Four Questions That Can Change Your Life*, Three Rivers Press, 2002.

Lang, M. D. & Taylor, A., *The Making of a Mediator: Developing Artistry in Practice*, Jossey-Bass, 2000.

Levinson, W. et al., 'Physician-Patient Communication: The Relationship with Malpractice Claims Among Primary Care Physicians and Surgeons', in: *Journal of the American Medical Association*, Vol. 277, No. 7, 1997.

Luskin, F., *Forgive for Good: A Proven Prescription for Health and Happiness*, HarperCollins, 2002.

Mayer, B., *The Dynamics of Conflict Resolution: A Practitioner's Guide*, Jossey-Bass, 2000.

Moore, C. W., *The Mediation Process: Practical Strategies for Resolving Conflict*, Jossey-Bass, 3rd Ed., 2003.

Rosenberg, M. B., *Nonviolent Communication: A Language of Life*, Puddle-Dancer Press, 1999.

Shell, G. R., *Bargaining For Advantage: Negotiating Strategies for Reasonable People*, Penguin Books, 2nd Ed., 2006.

Stone, D., Patton, B. & Heen, S., *Difficult Conversations: How to Discuss What Matters Most*, Penguin Books, 1999.

Thomas, K. W. & Kilmann, R. H., *Conflict Mode Instrument*, Xicom, 1974.

Ury, W., Brett, J. M. & Goldberg, S. B., *Getting Disputes Resolved: Designing Systems to Cut the Costs of Conflict*, Jossey-Bass, 1988.

Ury, W., *The Power of A Positive No*, Bantam Books, 2007.

Ury, W., *Getting Past No: Negotiating Your Way From Confrontation to Cooperation*, Bantam Books, 1993.

US Dept of Veteran's Affairs, *Impasse Breaking Techniques*, http://www.va.gov/ADR/Impasse.asp, 1 January 2013.

Vaughan, F. E., *Awakening Intuition*, Anchor Press, 1979.

Wilmot, W. & Hocker, J., *Interpersonal Conflict*, McGraw-Hill Education, 8th Ed., 2011.

Winslade, J. & Monk, G., *Narrative Mediation: A New Approach to Conflict Resolution*, Jossey-Bass, 2001.

Yarn, D. H., *Dictionary of Conflict Resolution*, Jossey-Bass, 1999.

Index

C

Cloke, Kenneth ('Ken') – ii, xviii, 41, 63, 119

closure – 123

Coleman, Peter – xviii

collaborate/collaboration/collaborative – 9, 10, **20**, 31, 33, 35, 36, 39, 40, 43, 47, 48, 55, 56, 63, 70, 86, 94, 106, 108, 118, 125, 133, 136, 158, 195

Collaborative process guide, not decision maker (mediator's stance) – 10, **20**

communication – 6, 8, 16, 17, 20, 22, 24, **43-52**, 54, 55, 57, 69, 72, 74, 80, 103, 132, 137, 138, 152, 153, 154, 155

competition/competitive – 20, 33, 35, 39, 40, 48, 56, 65, 106, 108, 109

compromise – 33, 35, 37

conciliation/conciliatory – xiv, 3, 40, 53, 54, 79, 85, 86, 98, 159

confidences – 10, 17, 21, 22, 60, 73, 146

conflict(s) – 1, 2, 4, 5, 6, 7, 19, 20, 21, 26, 27, 28, 29, 30, 32, 33, 34, 35, 36, 37, 40, 41, 46, 47, 48, 55, **56-57**, 58, 65, **69**, 89, 95, 102, 103, 104, 112, 116, 119, 120, 123, 124, 125, 130, 131, 133, 137, 140, 151, 157, 158, 194, 195

conflict resolution – 1, 2, 7, 20, 21, 26, 41, 46, 56, 102, 132, 195

contempt – 14, 15, 29, 166

convening – **62**, 63, 137

convening caucus – 60, 65, 70, **130-133**, 140, 141

costs – **117**, 186

court(s) – xiii, xiv, 4, 6, 7, 57, 97, 110, 112-113, 114, 116, 122, 157, 158

creative – iv, 7, 9, 25, 40, 47, 48, 52, 66, 91, 92, 93, 99, 107, 120, 123, 153, 157, 162

customer service – 195

D

Damasio, Antonio – xviii

Dana, Daniel – xvii, 85, 98, 123, 125, 133, 134

decision(s) – 3, 10, 20, 25, 28, 29, 40, 41, 46, 50, 56, 63, 64, 70, 71, 115, 116, 137, 142, 155, 163, 164, 166, 174, 175

demands – 37, 47

differences/different – 10, 23, 24, 100, 157, 169

discipline – **100**

discrimination (or harassment) – 4, 99, 101, 102, 109, 112, 118, 128, 141, 147, 149

disgust – 14, 29, 164, 165, 166

dispute(s) – 3, 35, 39, 54, **56-57**, 97, 100, 104, 111, 112, 119, 126, 128, 157, 158, 195

doubt – 29, 48, 71, 104, 114, 115, 137, 158

E

Ekman, Paul – xix, 14, 29, 164

elicit – 73

e-mail(s) – 125, 126, 144, 149, 151, 154, 168

H

happiness – 14, 29, 31, 93, 164, 166
harassment – 22, 99, 101, 102, 161
hearing(s) – xvi, 1, 4, 86, 88, 147, 151, 160, 161
Helie, John – xviii, xix
hope – xvii, 2, 10, 18, 24-25, 36, 47, 51, 57, 61, 67, 68, 72, 75, 111, 120, 143, 146, 150, 151, 155, 156, 157, 158
humor – i, 16, 22, 86

I

identity – xviii, 5, 10, 34, 37, 78, 91, 116, 119, 124, 139
impasse – 59, 107, 119, 120, 121
implicit – 32, 136
influence – 17, 24, 29, 49, 51, 77, 81, 85, 118, 119, 164
information – 32, 96, 152, 163
Inspiring beacon of hope (mediator's stance) – 10, **24-25**
interests – 17, 31, 37, 47, 63, 115, 149, 174
Interpersonal Conflict (by Wilmot and Hocker) – xviii, 186
intervene/intervention – xv, 3, 5, 10, 13, 44, 51, 55, 56, 59, 60, 63, 66, 69, 73, 78, 79, 80, 86, 88, 95, 109, 158
investigation(s) – xvi, 1, 4, 6, 7, 22, 31, 83, 96, 101, 102, 158
issue(s) – xvi, 5, 7, 23, 32, 34, 36, 47, 49, 52, 56, 61, 65, 77, 79, 80, 95, 96, 98, 100, **102-104**, 107, 115, 117, 119, 120, 124, 125, 133, 137, 140, 153, 157 159, 162, 169, 173, 174, 181
'I' statements – **49**, 50, 132, 143

J

job security – 100, 114, 153
joint meeting/session – 59, 60, 86, 88, 108, 111, 117, 133, 135

K

Keeper of confidences (mediator's stance) – 10, **21-23**
Kilmann, Ralph – 33

L

learning – **99**, 163, 185
listen/listening – ii, 6, 14, 17, 18, 19, 43, 44, 47, 63, 64, 69, 78, 79, 82, 91, 119, 131, 132, 135, 137, 162, 167

M

Mandela, Nelson – xiv
mask – 10, 11, 15
Mayer, Bernard – xviii

mediator's stance – ii, 7, 9, **10**, 27, 55, 56, 65, 71

Melamed, Jim – xviii, xix, 106, 162

memory – 31

model – iii, 12, 17, 20, 27, 36, 43, 49, 64, 69, 194

money – 100, 163

Moore, Christopher – xviii

Most Likely Alternative to a Negotiated Agreement (MLATNA) – 114, 122

N

Namibia – xiii, xiv, xv, 195

needs – xviii, 2, 4, 5, 6, 13, 20, 21, 24, 26, 29, 31, 35, **36-39**, 44, 46, 47, 48, 49, 50, 58, 63, 65, 78, 82, 89-91, 92, 94, **95-99**, 106, 107, 113, 116, 117, 118, 119, 124, 152, 153, 157, 158, 162, **163**, 164, 167, 168, 169

negative attributions – 62

negotiation – xi, xvi, 2, 8, 20, 26, **35**, 36, 39, 53, 55, 56, 59, 60, 62, 77, 89, 92, 95, 105, 106, 107, 108, 112, 113, 114, 118, 119, 123, 126, 130, 132, 154, 157, 174, 195

'no' – 11, 49, 50, 83

Northern California Human Resources Association (NCHRA) – 195

O

objective criteria – 125

offer(s) – ii, iii, 4, 10, 13, 30, 41, 57, 87, 98, 108, 109, 112, 115, 121, 134, 142, 178

opening statement – 7, 8, 58, 60, 62, **66**, 67, 68, 70, 71, 73, 74, 75, 79, 133, 144, 145

Open to subtle information and feedback (mediator's stance), 10, **13-16**

option(s) – 6, 36, 59, 73, 86, 91, **92-96**, 101, 108, 114, 115, 118, **153-154**, 157, 173, 181

orange (illustrative story – conflict prevention and meeting needs) – 37

origin (national) – 101

P

passive-aggressive – 12, 87, 117, 151

patience – 33, 52, 79

pause – 51, 120

peace/peaceful – ix, 2, 21, 157, 163, 194, 195

performance – 32, 55, 90, 96, **100-101**, 108, 111, 118, 127, 132, 137, 139, 140, 141, 142, 143, 144, 147, 148, 149, 151, 152, 153, 154, 155, 167, 168, 176

perspective – ii, 7, 21, 43, 44, 58, 70, 76, 77, 78, 79, 81, 82, 97, 100, 113, 131, 133, 139, 141, 145, 147, 148, 149, 162

plan – xiv, 13, 101, 121, 150, 155

policy – 1, 4, 6, 7, 22, 100, 102, 108, 111, 140, 160

positive – 29, 31, 41, 45, 46, 47, 48, 50, 79, 86, 99, 100, 164, 169, 194

post-investigation – xvi, 102

posture(s) – 7, 9, 18, 45, 98, 120

power – 20, 34, 36, 40, 41, 70, 107, 109, **118**, 119, 149, 157, 160

About the Author

John Ford, BA LLB (UCT) is an experienced workplace mediator and soft-skills trainer.

John studied law at the University of Cape Town before moving to Namibia, where he practiced from 1988 to 1995. Initially, he focused on representing survivors of human-rights abuses. After Namibian independence in 1990, his focus shifted to labor and employment law.

John moved to California in 1996 and trained as a mediator. He has since successfully mediated hundreds of workplace disputes, and has worked with numerous teams to help them deal successfully with conflict.

John has provided training to thousands of employees at all levels in the workplace, across a wide range of industries. His workshops focus on the development of soft skills, such as communication, negotiation, facilitation, conflict resolution, emotional intelligence, customer service and mediation.

John teaches negotiation at UC Berkeley School of Law, mediation to graduate Business and Psychology students at Golden Gate University, and organizational collaboration online through Creighton University.

He is a past president of the Association for Dispute Resolution of Northern California (ADRNC), and was the managing editor of www.mediate.com from 2000 to 2011. Currently, he is a member of the Association for Conflict Resolution and the ADRNC.

John is the current trainer of a two-day Mastering Workplace Mediation seminar for members of the Northern California Human Resources Association (NCHRA). He also teaches a longer version of this class through UC Berkeley Extension. It is this training and his passion to make the world a more peaceful place that inspired him to write this book, and more recently to found the HR Mediation Academy.

John Ford and Associates: www.johnford.com

Our goal is to support organizations to approach inevitable internal workplace conflict with greater clarity and confidence.

We want you to feel comfort – not dread and fear – and be at ease when thinking about the way conflict is handled at your organization.

We want to support your organization to be conflict-resolution competent, which involves:

- knowing how to identify conflict early so you can nip it in the bud
- having simple tools to de-escalate, not escalate, conflict
- having a clear path to the lasting resolution of conflict.

Beyond providing coaching and training that develop these vital workplace skills, we mediate when you want the benefit of an external professional.

Our ultimate goal, however, is to support you and your organization to know what to do yourselves. We believe that HR professionals are required to be conflict-resolution competent. And, of course, employee-relations specialists need to be experts!

The HR Mediation Academy: www.hrmediationacademy.com

This is a specialized division of John Ford and Associates. It provides knowledge and skill-development opportunities aimed at supporting HR Managers who want to mediate workplace conflict themselves. In order to accomplish this, we offer both face-to-face and online training.

The HR Mediator Blog: www.thehrmediator.com

This blog is dedicated to spreading the word about internal workplace mediation. It aims to inspire HR Managers who want to make the world a more peaceful place, starting with the opportunities provided by their workplace.

Made in the USA
Las Vegas, NV
21 January 2022